PROPERTY

M. A. DONOHUE & CO., PRINTERS AND BINDERS, CHICAGO

CONTENTS

By Arthur Jerome Eddy

"The Law of Combinations."

"Two Thousand Miles on an Automobile."

"Delight, the Soul of Art."

"Recollections and Impressions
    of James A. McNeill Whistler."

"Ganton & Co."

"Tales of a Small Town."

"The New Competition."

"Cubists and Post-Impressionism."

PREFACE

The manuscript of the following pages was completed and prepared for publication just before the death of the author, which occurred in New York on July 21, 1920.

Any man who is concerned with the fundamentals of thought in any department — whether in philosophy, morals, politics, religion, the physical sciences, or art — grows weary of the multitude of books which only thresh over again the straw of old ideas, and contribute nothing of vitally new suggestion toward solving the problems of our life. But now and again it happens that one comes upon a book which bears the impress of really independent vision and original thought. Then one knows that one has found a teacher, a leader.

Such a teacher and intellectual leader was Arthur Jerome Eddy. The originality of his ideas is as surprising as the ease and clearness with which he expressed them, and the number of fields in which he was a master.

His leading quality was a certain alert openness of soul, a youthful responsiveness to the challenge of new ideas, new experiments, new valuations. His writings are full of this spirit of generous acceptance, balanced by a splendid sanity, which never allowed the enthusiasm of welcome to overbear a sound critical judgment.

So intensely individual is his method of analysis that the reader feels as though he were seeing for the first time the subject of which the author treats. His books on economic and social problems, and their ethical implications, carry to the mind of every instructed reader the conviction of their large and lasting significance.

In *The New Competition,* and in this book on *Property,* Mr. Eddy recognizes many evils that the conservative is usually unwilling to admit. He condemns many existing practices in business as being immoral, inhuman, and at the same time uneconomic, inefficient, and unnecessary. He would probe the conscience of the man of business. He will not tolerate the perpetuation of the standards of the jungle, nor permit men to defend them by the parrot-cry that struggle is the law of life. But instead of counselling the destruction of the entire competitive system and the substitution of some new and inherently unworkable scheme, woven out of the large inexperience of the utopist, Mr. Eddy challenges the existing order *to do what it claims to do,* and to show its capacity for self-reformation.

His remedy for many of the underhanded tricks that still prevail in the industrial world is simply *open competition* — honorable rivalry on the basis of full exchange of information among the competitors *and their customers and employees.* He would move in the opposite direction to that which the law so unfortunately followed when it undertook, by the Sherman Act and subsequent legislation, to perpetuate competition of the jungle type, and prevent, in ordinary businesses, that rational cooperation which the law itself has since been compelled to establish among the railroads.

The underlying principle of Mr. Eddy's theories of competition and property is this — that all business exists *for the service of the community.* Certain great human needs must be met, either by the voluntary labor and cooperation of individuals, or by the action of the community through the state. The socialist would have the state do everything. His opponent maintains that the community is bet-

ter served by what is called "private enterprise," because, in the latter, those who undertake the service assume the risk. Their own
success or failure is inexorably bound up with
that of their undertakings. The blunders and
miscarriages of the state do not involve the
loss and failure of the officials responsible for
them. The money used in state undertakings
is not the property of those who handle it.
That is why they are, in general, careless, lax,
and wasteful in their dealings with it.

Mr. Eddy is at his best in dealing with the
alleged "natural right" to property. His
criticism of Henry George's attempt to establish a distinction between property in land and
property in things is, to my thinking, unan-
swerable. There is no "natural right" to
property of any description. The right to any
property whatsoever is conferred by society.
Its basis is not in nature, but in social expediency. The community permits each of us to
enjoy exclusive control over certain parcels of
land and things because — and only because — *it*
gets more efficient service out of such land and
things than it otherwise could.

Mr. Eddy's strength, and that which con-

stitutes his clearest title to a hearing, is the
fact that, being an idealist, he was also a man
of immense practical experience. A lawyer by
profession — declared by the highest authorities
to have been one of the most brilliant at the
American bar — he had devoted years of work
to the organization of great business undertakings. He pointed out the path on which
advance is actually taking place. He was no
unpractical radical theorist.

His finest insight is his clear perception that
the evils which afflict society are, after all, due
not to external conditions, but to unpurged
defects in human nature itself. He is well
aware that these defects would produce similar
or worse evils in any system that could con-
ceivably be substituted for the present one.
Deceit, unfair competition, stupidity, underhanded dealing, inhuman lack of consideration
for one's neighbor — these are faults inherent in human nature, not in "capitalism." They
are not produced by the profit-seeking motive,
nor are they remedied by merely taking that
motive away. Human nature, with its faults and
virtues, is vastly independent of its surroundings. It makes them; it is not made by them. It

can vitiate or ennoble any social, industrial, or political order. *Expellas furcâ* — even the *furca* of communism or socialism — *tamen usque recurret*.

The appreciation of Mr. Eddy's teachings, and his fame as a constructive thinker, will continue to increase as his thought — so far in advance of his time — conquers the attention to which its worth entitles it.

To all who knew him, Mr. Eddy's death was an inexpressible personal loss; to his country it was the loss of a great intellectual and moral asset. From such radiant spirits as his we catch the faith that makes progress possible.

HORACE J. BRIDGES.

CHICAGO, *June, 1921.*

PROPERTY

chist, does not shrink from this conclusion—
that *progress* and our entire *civilization* are
based upon injustice.[1]

But, how can justice come out of injustice?
How can *progress* come out of *wrong?*

The very terms of the question force the conclusion that we are deceived regarding either
the *wrong* or the *progress*.

If there has been *true progress* its basis has
been *right;* if the fundamental institution of
society—property—is *really wrong* then there
has been no true progress.

There are three ways out of the dilemma:

1. Property is right and progress real.

2. Property is wrong and progress unreal.

3. Property is both right and wrong;
progress is both real and unreal.

Most men argue so strongly in favor of the
first proposition that property rights are held

---

[1] It should be noted and conceded in passing that the
debate often turns on the definition and conception of the
word " progress "—one side taking it in its mere material
sense, the other in its more cultural and ideal sense, deny-
ing the world has spiritually and ideally progressed notwithstanding its apparent material prosperity; obviously
that debate admits of no definite conclusion, it being a
conflict of sentiments, opinions, convictions.

by them to be *sacred,* almost as sacred as a man's right to his life.

Comparatively few men argue in favor of the second proposition; even Proudhon was obliged to admit that though he considered property theft, still it was an institution that could not be disturbed suddenly.

An increasing number of thinkers hold that while the institution of property has been on the whole a vital factor in the progress of mankind it is by no means perfect, and, like *every social institution,* is open to *criticism* and *correction.*

❖ ❖ ❖

In short, property is not the evil it is said to be, otherwise progress would not be so real as it undoubtedly has been.

On the other hand true progress may have been checked because of *imperfect* or *over-*recognition of property rights.

All of which leads to the *conclusion* that the first duty of the man who would reform society is to *clear up his ideas* regarding property.

It is easy enough to say, "Property is theft," but difficult to prove the assertion.

It is easy enough to say, "Property is sacred," but equally difficult to prove it so.

The truth probably lies between the two extreme positions — property is neither theft nor sacred, it is just *human,* and, like all things human, imperfect.

❖ ❖ ❖

To say "Property is theft," is like saying "Law is crime." But every paradox contains some truth.

❖ ❖ ❖

At the very outset of any consideration of the matter of accumulation and distribution of wealth, we are met by prejudices that stand in the way of cool, patient, and thorough investigation.

The greatest of these prejudices is that of the man who has less against the man who has more *simply because he has more.*

The names of Rothschild and Rockefeller are sweet morsels in the mouth of the *ranting* socialist, communist, and anarchist; the *philosophical* socialist, communist, and anarchist should be above that sort of thing, but even he cannot refrain from pointing to some huge fortune as if *mere size* of some man's fortune added force to his argument.

Logically speaking whether a man has a billion, or a million, or ten thousand matters not so long as he has more than the average.

In fact a billion in the United States may mean less to the community than a hundred thousand in a remote colony.

❖ ❖ ❖

The story is told that one day a man rushed up to Rothschild and exclaimed angrily:

" You have a million pounds."

" Well? "

" You've no right to so much money."

" Who should have it? "

" The people."

" Of England or the world? "

" Of — of the world," the man faltered.

"All right, take your share out of this and distribute the balance where it belongs," and the banker handed the man a penny.

❖ ❖ ❖

Rockefeller's alleged billion distributed among the people of the United States would give each man, woman, and child, less than ten dollars.

That would not go far toward eliminating poverty.

Then, too, by what *right* would the people of the United States *exclude* other nations and races from participating in the distribution? The money of the Standard Oil Company has been drawn from the four quarters of the globe.

And if the people of the United States may exclude other nations and races from participating, why may not the people of Ohio, where the company started, exclude the people of Illinois, Alaska, Hawaii?

❖ ❖ ❖

In the United States some cities and some states are far richer than others. In the world some nations and some lands are far richer than others.

If there is to be an equalization of wealth where shall the distribution end?

The people of New York State make their money with the aid and cooperation of not only all the other states but of Canada, Europe, and more distant countries.

The people of the United States accumulate wealth by the direct cooperation of all other peoples to the remotest races of darkest Africa.

Whatever our wealth, it is due to the exertions and sacrifices of others as well as ourselves.

It follows, therefore, that a *perfectly just* distribution cannot be made within the confines of a single nation, any more than within the confines of a single state, city, or village. The thorough-going communist must be consistent; he must urge the white farmers and workmen of the northern states to share their homes and farms with the ten million negroes of the South.

Between the existing distribution with all its inequalities and any scheme of distribution that falls short of taking into consideration *all* mankind the result would be simply a difference in the *degree* of *injustice*.

The most thorough-going communist is willing to divide his neighbor's goods, he may even be willing to divide his own — if he has any, but he is thoroughly *selfish* when it comes to sharing his country's goods with the rest of the world, with the millions of Asia and Africa, not to overlook the Esquimaux and South Sea Islanders, who are also our brothers in *theory* if not in law.

Communism, and most other projects for reform, begin and stop at home.

While the suggestion to distribute equally the wealth of the United States among the people of the United States may arouse some — not much as a matter of fact — interest among those who have less than the per capita average, it arouses no enthusiasm whatsoever among those who have more; while the suggestion that the distribution should be carried to its logical extreme and the wealth of this country be cast in one common fund for distribution to the entire world, would arouse simply ridicule.

In short it may be human nature to like to share the fortunes of others, but it is not human nature to cheerfully relinquish to strangers and enemies what we consider our own.

Ask the average farmer if he would favor dividing up Rockefeller's fortune among those who have less, and he might answer, " Yes."

Ask him if he would favor sharing his farm with those who have nothing and he would surely reply, " No."

❖ ❖ ❖

This human weakness in favor of despoiling the other fellow is illustrated in the provisions of the income tax laws of this and other countries, wherein small incomes are exempt or subjected to low taxes, and large incomes are progressively seized by ingeniously devised surtaxes.

Suggestions are made to so increase the surtaxes on incomes and estate or inheritance taxes as to practically confiscate large incomes and large fortunes. In other words to utilize the taxing power to equalize fortunes.

Most of these suggestions are opposed by reasoning that is far more fallacious than that urged in support of them. They are denounced as demagogical, which is true, but that charge is cheap, easily made and has nothing to do with the merits, if any, of the suggestions.

They are opposed as revolutionary, radical, socialistic, etc., etc., but these epithets simply obscure the real issue; they settle nothing.

Not a few objections are based upon a denial of the government's *right* to confiscate all or a portion of a man's income, but that position is hopelessly untenable. If the government can collect a graduated income tax, increasing from one to sixty per cent, it can make the graduation from one to one hundred per cent. There is no limit to the *right*.

Constitutional objections might be urged in this country, but such objections at most would simply mean the amending of constitutions, and the definite assertion of rights denied.

The power resides in the people and they may do as they please with laws and constitutions.[1]

---

[1] Here again is a generalization that would require a small volume to qualify properly. Profoundly speaking it is far from true to say "the power resides in the people to do as they please with laws and constitutions." It is even truer to say "the people are *powerless* to do as they please with laws, constitutions, institutions," as powerless as they are to alter their language, habits, modes of thought, etc., overnight. We live under governments and social conditions that have slowly developed through the centuries. We may jostle them by revolutions, we may

The man who asserts his *right* to hold either all or any part of his property, on the ground the community has *no right* to interfere with him, destroys the basis of his argument in that he takes away the very foundation of all rights the assent of the community.

If no better arguments can be urged in favor of large incomes, then those who have them might just as well make up their minds to lose them. *But the reason why large incomes have not been confiscated long ago is because there are economic reasons for their existence,* and these reasons have controlled throughout the ages, though — curiously enough — they have never been systematically set forth.

If "swollen fortunes" — as the phrase goes — are an economic evil it is *clumsy* and *ineffective* to attempt to remedy the evil by such crude devices as inheritance and income taxes;

modify them by wise action, but to say they are subject to our will, our caprice, is to say what is obviously not so. However, for the purposes of the argument in this book it may be conceded the people have the power to do as they please with laws, constitutions, institutions, that they may do what they please regarding all so-called property rights.

as clumsy and ineffective as if the state attempted to remedy *piracy,* not by suppressing it, but by taking part of the *plunder.*

The " swollen fortune " is a *fact* in our *economic development.*

There may be but one *billionaire* but there are any number of *millionaires,* thousands of *hundred-thousandaires* and hundreds of thousands *ten-thousandaires.*

From the point of view of the man who has nothing, an American farmer with ten thousand has a " swollen fortune," and it is swollen far beyond the farmer's *pro rata* share of the country's wealth.

The " swollen fortune " is not a thing of absolute magnitude, but entirely a matter of comparative size.

❖ ❖ ❖

To repeat:

Inequality in the distribution of wealth is a *fact,* a very stubborn fact, in the economic development of *all* mankind.

There has never been a time in the history of the human race when some individuals did not have more than others.

To find anything like a theoretical holding of things in common one must resort to the insect world, and even there and in the animal kingdom there is a more or less well-defined assertion of ownership by the individual or the colony to the exclusion of others, even to the killing and slaughtering of others.

Even a theoretically pure communism could not avoid the following *inequalities* in the distributions of the accumulated wealth of the community:

A. The wealth of one community as compared with the wealth of other nations, peoples, and races.

B. The greater wealth of some localities as compared with that of others.

C. Inequalities in the distribution of community advantages, such as public buildings, properties, industries necessarily localized, railroads, highways, universities, museums, etc., etc.

In short the most abstractly ideal community could not surround each individual with *precisely the same* convenience and comforts. How to deal with those individuals who do the hard

and dirty work and place them on a plane of
equality with those who do the light and pleas-
ant has troubled every philosopher who has
ever tried to devise a utopia; if you give them
larger returns inequality immediately results
—the adjustment would be impossible.

If the ideal community should make its capital or any one city more attractive than another, or should indulge in a single expense for
the purpose of making life more agreeable in
any locality, or more agreeable for one man,
woman, or child than for another there is *inequality* of *distribution* of advantages which is
practically the same as, and theoretically, more
unjust than, inequality in the distribution of
private property.

All *dreams* of great and glorious communities, states, commonwealths, wherein private
property does not exist, and everything is held
in common, *involve* inequalities in the distribution of *advantages* and *pleasures* that are fully
as great as any that now exist.

That is to say, the *greater* the *glories* of the
utopia the greater the concentration of advan-

tages in favored localities — in the spotlights
of the dream. A utopia with no concentration
of advantages, no great cities, no great buildings, monuments, museums, pleasure resorts,
theaters, orchestras, etc., etc., would not be a
utopia to fire the imagination.

It must not be forgotten that to the man in
the coal mine, to the man ploughing the field,
to the negro in the cotton fields, to the miner
in Alaska, to the sailor, the fisherman, the
stoker in the hold, the collector of garbage, all
the gorgeous and beautiful buildings, amusements, and enterprises of the utopian common-
wealth would be as remote and unrelated as
are the buildings and pleasures of existing
states and commonwealths; they would read of
them but never enjoy them.

Furthermore it must not be forgotten in this
connection that *inequality is the law of life.*

Perfect equality, if attainable, would mean
stagnation, death; a placid, rippleless sea; a
currentless, motionless air; a still and silent
universe.

The slightest action, change, growth, development, means disturbance of equality.

It is idle to talk of equality between youth and age, men and women, race and race, the feeble and the strong, the fool and the wise man.

The truth is two human beings cannot be found who are equal in all respects, equal in physical and mental equipment; in desires, emotions, impulses; above all in those subtle qualities that go to make up what we call *personality*.

Thinking men who admit this seek refuge from the consequences of the admission by saying that what is meant by " equality " is *" equality before the law,"* a sounding phrase that is used to discourage further inquiry and analysis, but which means nothing.

Men are no more equal before the law than in other respects, and to the extent the law treats them as equal, recognizes no distinction between the weak and the strong, the stupid and the intelligent, the confiding and the crafty, to that extent is the law both blind and deficient.

The law commits its most frightful errors when it fails to take into consideration the personal equation.

❖ ❖ ❖

The men who are most virulent against inequality of wealth are usually quite complacent toward inequality of *authority;* many of them claim and exercise the most *despotic authority* over their followers; *all* of them are most *intolerant* of opinions that differ from their own.

Karl Marx, for instance, was so intolerant of opposition or rivalry that when his control of the International Workingmen's Association was threatened he deliberately wrecked the Association.

As between inequality measured in *dollars* and inequality measured in authority, the latter has probably done the world incomparably more harm—and good.

The power of the man of money over the man who has none is nothing as compared with the power of the man who has will-power over the man who has none—the latter is the blind and helpless slave of the former, to the doing of murder.

Of all dogmatic and tyrannical teachers of men, the socialists, anarchists, and radical reformers generally, have ever been and are the most intolerant and despotic.

Leaders of labor unions exercise powers that few generals on a battle field possess, for troops may hang back or run, but unionists seldom fail to strike, fight, and starve at the command of their leaders.

The point of all this is that inequality is not confined to the distribution of wealth; *it exists everywhere,* in the family, the school, the church, the city, the state; in politics and in every profession; some men get on faster than others, and the great majority in every walk of life is ever looking up to and following a small minority, and, it is a curious fact, in every walk of life except that of making money, the majority is *proud* of the achievements of the minority—proud of the inequality that distinguishes the leaders.

The unknown doctor, lawyer, minister, professor, does not desire the levelling of the famous members of his profession; his one ambition is to achieve something of their success.

The workman in a factory does not desire the levelling of the foreman, the superintendent, the men who are above him by reason of their ability to direct; on the contrary he is ambitious to advance to their positions.

Government employees range in rank from the president down to the humblest janitor, but not a soul in the employ of the government dreams of the possibility of the levelling of all ranks, of the arbitrary placing of the janitor on the same level of pay and authority with the president; on the contrary the normal ambition of all is to *rise* from rank to rank — in short to systematically perpetuate the scheme of inequality.

No socialistic community has ever been suggested wherein there would not be the same gradations of office and authority, the same *inequalities* between man and man, and the same rivalry and strife to *advance* in rank and authority.[1]

---

[1] The late Czar exercised no such despotic power as that wielded by Lenine and Trotsky. And so far from abolishing classes, the Russian revolution has simply created an interest-

At most the socialist and communist would simply level *some* of the inequalities of wealth.

Well, inequalities of wealth are among the *least* of the world's troubles.

Inequalities of wealth alone have never produced a revolution, never overturned a government, never caused a war.[1]

Inequalities of rank, power, privilege, are the inequalities that stir men to revolution and bloodshed. Inequalities of wealth may, and usually do, accompany these other inequalities; but not always and necessarily, and *never* as a *cause*.

Inequalities of rank, power, privilege, are *inherent* in men, in church and state, in labor unions and political parties, in sports and wars, and it is this *personal equation* that leads to inequalities in the distribution of wealth, and *not vice versa*.

In short, were it possible to correct today, by some magic stroke, all the inequalities in the distribution of *material things* — wealth — those

ing assortment of new ones.

[1] To this generalization — true as regards wealth generally — must be noted the exception of gross inequalities in *land ownership,* they do cause discontent of revolutionary magnitude.

other inequalities would instantly begin anew the work of *redistribution,* the stronger appropriating more or less of the *pro rata* share of the weaker; just as the head of any body — say the leader of a labor union — is paid more, and has more than any one of his followers, because his services are worth more and it is economy to make it an object to him to devote all his time to the organization.

It sometimes happens a great leader is willing to devote his energies to the state, to his organization, to a cause for the glory there is in the work and with no greater compensation than that of a day laborer, but these instances are *few* and as a rule his followers *will not permit it;* they instinctively recognize the truth that the power and efficiency of the leader depends not a little upon *appearances,* that he can do better work if he does not live as a day laborer, but keeps somewhat aloof. In other words a general's uniform is a time-saving device; without it the general would have to demonstrate his right to leadership to every new recruit. The policeman's badge saves a lot of questions.

The American people pride themselves on being democratic, yet they would not consider it wise or economical to have their President live in a three-room shack on the banks of the Potomac, or even in a six-room flat on one of the side streets of Washington, though in either case he might be consuming far more than his *pro rata* share of the wealth of the country.

Perhaps it is fortunate for those who enjoy inequalities of rank, power, privilege, that the minds of the people are diverted to the discussion of inequalities of wealth, for so long as *only* inequalities of wealth are assailed, the *unjustly powerful* are safe.

It is amusing to see how Congress and political bodies generally are quick to divert public attention from their own shortcomings by springing investigations of rich corporations and individuals.

No, the problem is profounder than the mere distribution of dollars.

❖   ❖   ❖

The fatal defect of every utopian community devised by philosopher or dreamer is

that it is based on the assumption of *physical,*
mental and *emotional equality* of individuals,
whereas the *truth* is that men and women are
all born helpless and many grow up so helpless
and incompetent that as against them the
others must assert authority over their food,
clothing, property, even their persons. So that
in even the *ideal* community the rights of individuals to participate in the control and distribution of property depend first of all upon *age;*
secondly, upon a development of *physical,*
mental and *moral* strength — three vital factors, concerning which the judgment of the
active majority is *conclusive.*

Rights, then, are of *practical* origin and
development rather than of *theoretical.*

It is easy to lay down *abstract* propositions
of great beauty and *seeming* truth, but men
differ so widely in their physical, mental and
moral attributes that the abstract propositions
do not fit.

Imagine a community wherein all persons
were of the *same* physical, mental and moral
development, possessed the *same* rights — equal

to no rights at all; wherein there was no need
for government, because of no human weaknesses and shortcomings; wherein there were
no strifes, struggles, failures, successes, but
life was one long, bright June day—life in
such a community would be so deadly monotonous it would not be worth living.

❖ ❖ ❖

But, though we assume that on account of
man's imperfections *inequality of fortune* is an
economic condition that is essential to *economic
progress,* it by no means follows that such
inequality is a *good* thing to be encouraged; on
the contrary, as it is the direct outcome of the
weaknesses and imperfections of mankind it
should be minimized, or at least confined within
as narrow limits as human imperfections admit.

Private property, with its resulting inequality
in the distribution of wealth, is essentially a
human institution in the same sense government is a human institution, and like the degree
of government its development depends entirely
upon human necessities. There is nothing
sacred about it, it is subject to the will of man,
and the very fact that man *has not abolished* it

long ago, notwithstanding the railings and arguments against it, is proof positive that he knows of no better device to take its place.

Private property is not a *popular* institution from the point of view of the masses, but it is inevitable, and even the masses have their property rights which they would not surrender without a fight.

❖   ❖   ❖

We have, then, this curious condition, one of the basic institutions of society is denounced as responsible for most of the miseries of life.

The appeal of the demagogue, of the socialist, of the economist, of the utopian philosopher is based upon a denunciation of private property. To be sure no two of these men agree in their arguments, their conclusions, or their remedies, but all agree in the assertion that there is *something wrong* with the institution of *private ownership*.

Where so many different thinkers are of one mind regarding a given institution it is only fair to concede there may be some foundation for their conviction, and if there is anything wrong with private ownership that wrong should be discovered and remedied.

There is, however, this alternative, the institution of private property *may not be thoroughly understood;* it may be charged with faults that do not exist, with evils for which it is not responsible.

❖ ❖ ❖

The prejudice against private property rests upon the assumption that one man has more than he ought to have, that in some way he *owns* and *makes use of* the fruits of the labors of others, for his own benefit or pleasure.

It is easy to stir the resentment of men who have nothing against men who have, by telling the former they have been robbed.

It is easy to sow hatred in a community by telling those of small means they would have more if the wealth of the few were fairly distributed.

Those have been the stock arguments of the demagogue throughout the ages, and it goes without saying, if the arguments were sound, private property would have disappeared long ago — or rather it never would have come into existence as a normal factor in social evolution.

One might just as well argue against the institution of government, of organized society. In spite of the strongest theoretical objections government and organized society are the best devices of the ages to meet and cope with human imperfections and dependencies.

Taking private property as it is established and protected in all civilized communities, and especially in the United States, the object of this little book is to try and find out *what it really is,* and *what is wrong with it.*

II

THE AVERAGE FORTUNE

Mr. John D. Rockefeller is said to have a fortune of a billion dollars. That is probably an exaggeration, but whether he has a billion or half a billion answers as well for the purposes of the argument.

According to the Census Bureau the average wealth of each man, woman, and child in the United States in 1910 was $1,300.

Mr. Rockefeller $1,000,000,000
Average person   1,300

Such statistical comparisons are easily and often made for the express purpose of arousing discontent and resentment, but—as will be found on analysis—the figures are quite misleading.

❖   ❖   ❖

A distinguished political leader is quoted as having said, "A man may *fairly earn* a million dollars."

The ideal millionaire $1,000,000
Average person   1,300

28

What is the difference between Mr. Rockefeller and the *ideal* millionaire?

Simply a difference in degree.

❖ ❖ ❖

The political leader referred to is said to have accumulated a fortune of over one hundred thousand dollars.

Leader $100,000
Average person   1,300

❖ ❖ ❖

The disparity is still enormous.
To recapitulate:

Mr. Rockefeller $1,000,000,000
Ideal millionaire   1,000,000
Political leader   100,000
Average person........   1,300

It may be said once for all that names are used in this book *solely* for the purpose of making the argument more vivid and with no thought of reflecting upon any man.

The point of importance here is the simple statistical proposition that to the extent any individual in the country has a fortune of *more* than $1,300, to that extent must others have less—hence the *seeming* extremes of wealth and poverty.

The word *"seeming"* is used advisedly for if the extremes of wealth and poverty were *actually* such as those indicated on the face of the statistics this country would be in the midst of a social upheaval such as the world has never known.

Or, to state the matter differently, it is inconceivable that a community of intelligent, self-governing people should tolerate social and economic conditions that permit one man to accumulate and *absolutely control* a million or a thousand times as much as another who is equally industrious and equally honest, but who may lack in executive ability.

Granting that executive ability, rare genius for invention or organization, is entitled to its reward, that it pays the community to encourage the exercise of such ability for the sake of the good reaped by the entire community, the proposition that such reward should be carried to the extent it *seemingly* is on the face of the statistics violates one's sense of justice.

If the *apparent* extremes of great wealth and abject poverty *shock every man's sense of what is fair,* why has the community tolerated the development of those seeming extremes?

And why does not the community remedy conditions which *on their face seem* so outrageously inequitable?

There are two possible answers to those questions:

1. The inequalities are as real as the figures indicate, but the community is too apathetic and slothful to remedy the wrong.

2. Inequalities exist, but by no means to the extent indicated on the face of the figures; the community is restless and eager for social and economic reform, but is not revolutionary and anarchistic in its demands because it *feels* without fully comprehending that somehow the figures are misleading and it *sees* that the actual inequalities between the rich and the poor are not so great as indicated.

❖ ❖ ❖

Of the two hypotheses the first may be dismissed at once as not in keeping with the intelligence of this or any other civilized people. Inequalities in the distribution of wealth anything like those indicated *on the face* of the statistics would be remedied by *revolution.*

The very fact that nations pursue the fairly even tenor of their ways century after century is proof positive to the social philosopher that while things may be far from right they are not so wrong as the radical socialist, communist, or anarchist, would have us believe.

Therefore *it must be* that the inequalities complained of are more *apparent* than real, and to the extent they ought not to exist the community is slowly but surely remedying them.

This last hypothesis is the only one that is consistent with our respect for the intelligence of mankind and with any plausible theory of the gradual evolution of all things social.

The very fact that social unrest in most countries, conspicuously in the United States, falls short of revolution is proof that the inequalities fall short of revolutionary magnitude. Per contra at the present moment the unrest in other countries since the World War, notably in Russia, has resulted in revolutions wherein the attempt is made to correct the inequalities of both wealth and power.

If the inequalities in the distribution of wealth were *actually* as great as indicated on the face of the figures quoted then Bolshevism not only *would* be, but *should* be rampant in the United States.

But if the conclusions regarding the *real* as distinguished from the *apparent,* or *seeming,* control and distribution of wealth are sound then it is certain that Bolshevism and the entire revolutionary propaganda—in so far as it attempts a redistribution of property—will subside after turning the limelight on many real evils, and after working many real reforms.

The man of philosophic mind watches with unprejudiced eye the spread of Bolshevism— i. e., radicalism—knowing that its vitality is measured by the truth it contains, and when that truth is exhausted—i. e. applied, demonstrated—the revolution, the movement, will necessarily come to an end.

The difference between the Bolshevik and the Menshevik—the radical and the moderate

—lies in the *extent* to which each would go in overturning existing institutions.

The Bolshevik sees little good in laws and institutions as they are and would overturn nearly everything. The Menshevik sees more good and would overturn less. It is idle to attempt to meet the arguments of either by denunciation. The only effective way is to listen dispassionately and analyze coolly but searchingly.

❖ ❖ ❖

So far as inequalities in the distribution of wealth are concerned the Bolshevik—the radical, the revolutionist—would seem to have it all his own way *on the face of the statistics.*

A billion, or a million, or even a hundred thousand to the average of thirteen hundred is not a comfortable comparison; while a billion or a million to nothing is a direct incentive to revolution.

❖ ❖ ❖

Do these figures accurately reflect the true conditions?

That is another of the questions we are going to try to answer.

III

Let us view the distribution of wealth from another angle.

Statistically and *legally* one man is a millionaire while another may have little or nothing.

The *inequality* between a million and one hundred or nothing is *enormous,* so enormous that only a mind accustomed to large figures can grasp it.

❖ ❖ ❖

While the *statistical* inequality between a *million* and a *few hundred* is enormous, *is it true* that the inequality *in real life* between the man who " owns " a million and the man who has but a hundred or even nothing is as enormous as the figures indicate? We have already committed ourselves to the proposition that *if it were* there would be *instant revolution;* which is equivalent to saying that social conditions would not tolerate the development of such monstrous conditions.

In a profound sense the " millionaire " is an *economic fiction;* one of the *illusions* incidental to economic progress. He exists in theory rather than in fact; he is a legal entity, rather than a living and breathing mass of gold, or wheat, or actual wealth of any kind.

❖ ❖ ❖

Take the present *instant,* the particular moment you — the reader — are reading this paragraph.

Pause and think.

All the people in the United States are *doing something,* most of them working hard.

Imagine yourself seated on a cloud taking a bird's-eye view of this country of ours.

Would it not resemble an ant-hill in activity? Would it not be true that the idlers, the wasters, the fools and criminals, who loom so large and make such an impression when close to us, would be so few they would be lost in the mass of workers?

Look more closely and try to distinguish, if you can, the millionaire from the thousandaire.

You do see that some dress better and live better than others, but these differences are measured not by millions but by a few hundreds annually.

The best buildings you find are public buildings, and some of those who have thousands per year are public servants; nearly all of the gorgeous uniforms, and many of the most extravagant entertainments, receptions, balls, parades, celebrations, etc., etc., are *public* functions, so that it is apparent the country — i. e., the community — not only countenances but *establishes* great *inequalities* in rank, power, office, salaries, comforts, luxuries, appearances, pleasures.

If you are of a reflective turn of mind you may ask yourself whether it may not be true that in these respects individuals simply ape the examples of states.

❖ ❖ ❖

Surveying from your seat on the cloud the *human ants,* who are, as a body, working so hard to accumulate wealth which *each generation must leave behind,* you notice all the *economic* inequalities in *distribution* and enjoyments above mentioned, and on the *human* side you observe physical, moral, intellectual differences which make certain economic inequalities inevitable. And the closer you look the more surprising it strikes you that *individuals* who differ so, one from another, in physical, moral and intellectual strength can get along so well together in one community.

❖ ❖ ❖

Now turn from the living units to the *results* of their labors, to the *total accumulated wealth* of the community from seed in the ground to finest finished products; from a path in the forest to an elaborately developed railway system; from a log cabin to the White House.

Your *first* and *absolutely correct* impression is that *all* this *wealth* belongs to the community —to the human ant-hill. You see that individuals are born and die, generations come and go, but the *economic* progress and accumulations of the community *go on* without interruption; it is all an essentially *community* proposition, differing only in degree and not in kind from the accumulations of the ant-hill and the beehive; a more complex and elaborate development of the tribal stage of mankind.

As a philosopher — particularly if a logical
evolutionist — you conclude at once that —
whatever the inequalities between individuals,
the *economic* system followed has been well
adapted to attain the results achieved. Given
any material changes in rights and incentives
it goes without saying the results would be
materially different — whether better or worse
no man can say, though the relentless logic of
evolution requires you to argue that the results
achieved are the *best possible* with an *imperfect* human factor; as the human factor gains
in physical, moral and intellectual strength,
material results will vary accordingly. If the
intelligence of some of the ants were doubled
the proportions of the hill would be changed.

❖   ❖   ❖

On closer study you find that individual members and groups of the community *assert claims*
to particular portions of the community wealth.

First of all the community itself is broken up
into many divisions and subdivisions, political,
religious, educational, industrial (such as public enterprises like gas, waterworks, irrigation
schemes, harbors, etc.) and that each of these

divisions *asserts a claim* to its special portion
of the total wealth.

This assertion *of claims* by the community
and by its various subdivisions, political and
industrial, does not alter *the fact* that every
building is used by and every public enterprise
run by *individuals*.

❖ ❖ ❖

By searching the *records* you ascertain the
legal fact that the White House is " owned "
by the nation, instead of by its occupant, but
this *legal* title does not alter the social fact it is
the home and office of an *individual,* the President, just as a house on Fifth Avenue may be
the home and office of a well-known physician.
The *legal title* to the house on Fifth Avenue
may be in the physician, or in his father, or in
a stranger, or a trust company, or in the City
of New York; it may change any moment without the physician knowing or caring, the
economic fact remains that the house is a part
of the sum total of community wealth and it is
occupied by a certain individual unit as a convenient place to best serve the community.

After ascertaining the *curious*—from your bird's-eye point of view—fact that the community as a whole, and many divisions of the community, claim legal title to portions of the community wealth, even to hundreds and hundreds of millions of gold stored in public vaults, you probe deeper and find:

That, following the example of the community, individuals and groups of individuals —from partnerships of two up to corporations with thousands of security holders—claim legal title to particular portions of the total wealth.

In short you find that:

1. The all-important and fundamental facts are, the production, use, and control of *all wealth* are by *individuals working in harmony.*

2. But, there are of *record* certain documents which give (a) the community, (b) political, religious, educational subdivisions of the community, (c) public corporations and enterprises, (d) semi-public corporations, (e) corporations, (f) associations of all kinds, (g) partnerships, (h) individuals, *legal title* to such

portions of the total wealth as they produce or
use, or " own " as the phrase goes.

This is a very *curious* and highly *artificial*
condition for it is at once apparent that if
every legal record *were burned* and no attempt
made to ascertain and restore the *legal* titles
not a penny of actual wealth would be affected,
and the only *occupations* of individuals that
would be affected would be those which had to
do with the preservation of these *legal* conditions and records. Aside from people engaged
in these occupations the work of every individual in the community would remain precisely the same *for a time*.

You naturally ask, " Why not, then, wipe out
this cumbersome *legal* machinery, and permit
the community to go along simpler economic
lines?"

The answer is twofold:

1. From the evolutionist's standpoint, it is
plain that cumbersome scheme of *legal* title, of
" ownership " as distinguished from actual use
and control, would not have developed unless
there was good reason for it. All civilizations

seem to have progressed in proportion to the extent they recognized and protected these *paper* property rights; the more elaborate the scheme of *paper* property rights the higher the civilization, and vice versa.

History proves the truth of this; it also shows that the recognition of rights — particularly political — may be carried so far the system totters and falls either by its own weight or by revolutions.

2. Aside from the cold materialistic conclusions of the evolutionist, it is apparent — the more you probe the matter — that this *legal notion* of ownership is the *most powerful incentive* to individual effort ever devised.

Possession is the most powerful incentive known to the *brute* mind, but the human has made a great advance over the brute in that it *separates* the *idea* of *ownership* from the *bald fact* of possession, and thereby *multiplies* indefinitely incentives to effort.

❖ ❖ ❖

The brute can *possess* but one or two things at a time; the *human* can " *own* "— have *legal title* — to many.

True, the human does not *possess* — occupy, or physically control — more than one or two, or at most a few, but because the *law* — i. e. the ingenious device of the community — says he may " own " more, and gives him the right to take possession (though often under great difficulties and restrictions), he is satisfied and goes on working feverishly to accumulate *paper titles* to things other individuals *possess* and *use.*

Were it not for this *invention* of *paper rights,* all incentive to production and accumulation would end near the brute level, namely with the production and accumulation of only so much as each individual could physically hold to the exclusion of others.

With the recognition — the invention — of paper titles the incentive to produce and accumulate is extended indefinitely.

❖ ❖ ❖

A most ingenious scheme to keep men at work. It is a direct appeal to the speculative instinct which is so powerful in — and peculiar to — mankind. It fosters and encourages the spirit of *accumulation,* permitting men to *think* they accumulate for themselves and their families, whereas in last analysis they simply swell the total accumulations of the community — the ant-hill.

It is a great *game*.

❖   ❖   ❖

The total *actual* wealth of the community is *one thing*, the *legal* or paper wealth is quite another.

Take a farm, for instance; there it is with its improvements and buildings. From your cloud perch you see every foot of the land, you see a family living in the house and several men working in the fields; it is all quite plain — as plain as an ant dragging food to its hill — these individuals are working a given piece of land for their own living and profit and thereby adding to the sum total of the wealth of the community.

Adjoining this farm is another, then another and another; then come forests, and mines, and factories, all worked by individuals who die and are succeeded by other individuals, and meanwhile the improvements go on, the sum total of the community wealth steadily increases until farms and mines and factories are exhausted then the individuals cannot produce so much during their lifetimes and the total wealth decreases.

All this is quite plain, but when you inquire closely *why* the individuals work so hard, why they try to produce so much more than each one consumes you hear of this scheme of " *ownership* " this *legal device* which permits a man to *say* he " owns " what others actually possess and use.

The farm you first looked at is not " owned " by the family or the men on it, it is " owned " by a man two thousand miles away, but while he — *A* — has the *legal title paper;* another man, *B,* has a *mortgage paper* of ten thousand dollars on the land and buildings; *C* has a chattel mortgage *paper* on the machines used; *D* has a *contract for purchase paper;* while *E,* the man with the family in the farmhouse, has a *lease paper.*

These are some of the ramifications of *paper* ownership — all *legal creations* as distinguished from *economic.*

Add together the various *values* placed upon

these various interests and the sum total would far exceed the actual value of the farm and its improvements.

Theoretically the two totals should coincide, but in practice they do not, as is amply demonstrated in almost every foreclosure where all the legal interests are merged by actual sale of property; there is usually a radical scaling down of *paper values,* and individuals who thought they were rich find themselves poor.

❖ ❖ ❖

Look at this great railroad running from New York to Chicago with its many tracks, stations, warehouses, cars, locomotives, etc. It is *all* in the *actual* possession of the thousands of employees, from president to flagman, who operate it.

Not one of those who actually control and operate the road could tell who the "owners" are, nor do they care so long as the owners do not interfere with efficient operation.

On inquiry you find that the road is *legally* "*owned*" by thousands of stockholders and, ahead of the stockholders, thousands of bondholders, many of whom have never seen any part of the line, and many of whom are women, children, banks, insurance companies, and other corporations, all of whom have pieces of paper which are their evidences of title.

All these pieces of paper could be burned without destroying a penny of actual wealth and without affecting in the slightest degree the daily duties of a single man or boy actually engaged in working the road—excepting, of course, those whose duties have to do with the issuing, signing, transferring of the pieces of paper—they would suddenly find themselves with nothing to do—but every other employee would go about his work just the same.

Just the same?

Not quite, for sooner or later they would all know that private ownership of the property had been abolished, that no more pieces of paper would be issued, and the entire service would take on the atmosphere of *state service,* an atmosphere of *listlessness* and *indifference,* the atmosphere of *routine,* of work with no expectations save that of slow advancement by seniority.

When you add together all the issues of stocks, bonds, notes, and other forms of indebtedness, evidenced by outstanding pieces of paper, the total is *so enormous* the question at once arises, "Is it possible the railroad is worth that much?"

Probably not, or if it is, it is due to the increased value of its franchise, right of way, terminals — *land values* — due to increase of population along the line rather than to actual labor and money put into the property, and besides much depends upon how " value " is defined, and by what rule " valuing " is done.

But whether the road is worth less or more than *all* its outstanding pieces of paper, the fact is obvious that there before your eyes is the physical property, the lines of rail, the stations, warehouses, cars, locomotives, etc., and there are the *workers* in *actual possession.*

In the hands of *others,* stockholders, bondholders, banks, etc., are pieces of paper which are bought and sold as valuable. One small stock certificate for two hundred shares may sell for more than a locomotive.

And because these pieces of paper *do sell* at

high prices there is a constant temptation to print more and more and more until confidence is shaken and the great structure of credit and inflation collapses. A drastic period of reorganization and readjustment follows. Fortunes and savings invested in the pieces of paper are lost. People are impoverished. But the road goes on just the same. Not a wheel ceases to turn, not an employee is laid off. It often happens that during these periods of destruction of paper values the road is rehabilitated and operated better than ever before. While paper values are tumbling, actual values, represented by labor spent upon the property, are increasing.

❖ ❖ ❖

We are so accustomed to *paper evidences* of wealth that we habitually confound them with actual wealth.

To the *farmer* the wheat stored in an elevator means more than the *warehouse receipt* issued against it, but to the banker the *piece of paper,* the receipt, means more than the wheat. The banker could not use a bushel of the wheat, but he will loan thousands of dollars on the piece of paper.

❖ ❖ ❖

So it is with notes, stocks, bonds, mortgages, the *pieces of paper* take the place of the real properties in all commercial and financial trans· actions, and the world comes to look upon them as if they were *actual wealth.*

❖ ❖ ❖

THEY ARE REAL IN THEIR WAY.

❖ ❖ ❖

That is the most important economic truth to get clearly in mind at the very outset of any investigation of real or apparent inequalities in the distribution of wealth.

❖ ❖ ❖

There are *enormous* inequalities in the distribution of *paper* wealth.

The inequalities in the distribution of *actual* wealth are *slight in comparison.*

We are getting close to the heart of the problem of the distribution of wealth.

The distribution of *actual* wealth is one thing.

The distribution of *paper* wealth is quite a different thing.

There are thousands and thousands of *paper* millionaires. There may be even a *paper* billionaire.

There is not and never has been an actual millionaire — *except*

    A. In *land*

    B. In *luxuries*

Both of which exceptions are fully considered in chapters ix and x.

It is a physical possibility for a man to "own" and have in his *exclusive* possession *paper* representing millions — hence he is a millionaire *on paper*.

It is — with the exception of *land* and *luxuries* — a physical impossibility for a man to " own " and have in his *exclusive* possession more than a few hundreds of thousands in *actual* wealth — hence he is *not* a millionaire when it comes to *actual* use and control of wealth to the *exclusion* of others.

The cry of the agitator, the argument of the socialist and communist are directed against the *paper millionaire.*

Little or no attention is paid to the *actual* —
i. e., the *land* or *luxury* millionaire.

It seems to be assumed that if a man is a
paper millionaire he will also be a land or
luxury (or both) millionaire.

It by no means follows.

If we exclude land millionaires who are in
an economic class by themselves the luxury
millionaires are comparatively few in numbers,
so few they are very conspicuous in the cities
where they live.

Most paper millionaires live in modest homes
and are known only as exceptionally hard
workers.   They go on all their lives accumulating these pieces of paper or enlarging their enterprises, spending little on themselves and
their homes.

❖ ❖ ❖

The trouble is not in the distribution of
paper wealth but in the distribution of *actual.*

True, inequalities in the distribution of paper
wealth may and often do lead to inequalities in
the distribution of actual, since paper wealth
is *power* over actual, but this power is not exer-

cised nearly so often as the agitator and the socialist think.

It is exercised so seldom that the cause of social, industrial, and commercial ills must be sought elsewhere.

And first of all in human nature itself.

That is the first great source of all our troubles — the weaknesses and vices of mankind.

Our institutions are no better than we are.

That is not quite true, for happily in a sense they are. Men preach better than they practice. Bad as they seem to be at times public — publicly professed — morals are *always* better than private. *We profess and uphold higher standards than we attain.* In politics and business we condemn practices we secretly follow.

Every community has hundreds of laws it cannot enforce, laws against drunkenness and prostitution, laws against unfair business methods, against cheating, deceiving, and fraud; pure food laws, laws for safety, hygiene, protection of women and children, and so on endlessly.

These laws are never enforced as fully as
they should be — why ?

Because the community cannot triumph over
the ingenuity and inherent waywardness of its
individual members.

❖ ❖ ❖

Every evil known to society has its origin in
and derives its strength from the individual.

When employers and employees are in violent
conflict, each side asserting the *rightness* of its
cause and conduct, the *thinking* man *knows*
that each side is made up of *men* equally
greedy, equally unscrupulous, equally quick to
fight, kill, burn — in short of men of the same
day and generation, just *average human
beings;* no white and spotless angels among
them.

❖ ❖ ❖

Conceding that the great source of all our
troubles, ethic as well as economic, is our own
imperfect human nature, still it does not follow
that we should fold our hands and sit supine.

On the contrary we have two tasks:

First, to hammer away with all our strength
at the weaknesses of our human nature, and

make ourselves better, so we may live up to
our standards—that is the *ethic,* and, if you
please, the physiologic task.

Second, to investigate profoundly and impar-
tially social and economic conditions with a
view to understanding and remedying them in
so far as imperfect human beings can remedy
inequalities that are so largely due to inherent
human imperfections—that is the *economic*
and *sociologic* task.

Inasmuch as these two *fundamentally distinct* conditions are at the base of all our
troubles it goes without saying that the reformer who promises his hearers perfection as
the result of the adoption of his economic or
social theories is promising something *that
cannot be.*

The socialist who draws a picture of social
contentment and happiness providing his suggestion of state ownership of capital be adopted
ignores completely the *human* factor, ignores
the physical, mental, moral, differences that
exist between man and man, nation and nation,
race and race.

His argument assumes that the adoption of an economic reform would instantaneously make imperfect men perfect. To bring the argument down to earth, it assumes that the moment the government takes over a given railway every employee instantly becomes an unselfish altruistic being whose sole thought is the welfare of humanity.

The hard cold fact is that labor unions in control of government enterprises are more selfish, more militant, more arbitrary, more aggressive than in privately conducted enterprises — as the recent experiment of government control of the railroads in this country has convincingly demonstrated.

❖   ❖   ❖

We have reached the conclusion that while the *nominal* or *legal* wealth of an individual may be very large, the *actual* wealth controlled or consumed by him may be relatively small.

A man may be *nominally* a millionaire or even a billionaire, and *actually* control and consume less wealth than a railroad president who has little besides his salary.

In fact the railroad president may actually

control and manage *productively* the wealth that is nominally and legally the property of the millionaire.

Take the extreme case of the millionaire who belongs to the " idle rich," who does nothing but amuse himself in ways that are productive of no good to the community.

This is an *extreme* hypothesis because even the most worthless and dissolute millionaire may build houses, improve estates, build yachts, buy fine homes or automobiles, and in his very extravagance unintentionally encourage the production of useful and beautiful things.

But take the extremest of extreme cases— the man whose very existence is a nuisance to the community and whose death would be a relief to family, friends, and the city in which he lives. The moral harm he does by his mode of life may be great, but that is a consideration by itself and applies to the poor man as well as the rich.

His *economic* cost to the community is the money he *wastes* on himself and others.

It would be interesting to analyze this term " waste," for it would be found that a certain percentage of the money spent in the most wasteful manner is not lost, but directly or indirectly benefits others. The moral evil of the expenditures may far overshadow the incidental economic benefit, but the benefit may be there just the same.

To state the proposition more baldly;

A rich man might take a cargo of wheat and sink ship and cargo in the middle of the ocean. That would be total loss to him and the community — absolute waste.

If instead of so doing he spent the value of the ship and wheat — say $200,000 in the wildest sort of riotous living, the moral example would be so bad the notoriety and shock might result in good; but *some* of the money would percolate back into productive channels; it would not be *all* lost as if the wheat were sunk in the ocean.

The worst economic effect of the wasteful spending would be to divert men and women for the time being from useful employments to the idle or vicious employments demanded by the spender.

There would be, however, at least some support and stimulation of occupations, trades, and industries of economic value to the community. The reckless buying of high-priced automobiles would be largely waste, but at the same time this reckless encouragement of automobile makers to exercise all their ingenuity to turn out more perfect, faster, and more elaborate cars, would stimulate the production of better cheap cars, just as the time and money formerly wasted in this country in horse racing was not wholly wasted since it helped perfect the breeds of horses for all purposes.

The yearly account of the worthless rich man with the community would stand as follows:

To the sum *total* of all the wealth consumed and spent — say.........$200,000
By so much of that amount as directly or indirectly advances useful employments — say............ 25,000

Annual cost to the community......$175,000

That is the item the community is interested in.

He may be "worth" ten million dollars. Suppose he inherited that amount. His income at only five per cent would be $500,000, three hundred thousand dollars of which he invests in more stock and bonds, because he cannot spend more than two hundred thousand dollars.

The public disapproves his way of living and rightly looks upon him as a nuisance, and because he is a vicious member of the community and spends lavishly he brings all millionaires into disrepute. The fault of the individual is attributed to his wealth, yet he is *not touching* a penny of his ten million dollars. Every dollar is productively engaged in the hands of others. If his fortune consists of railroad stocks his very existence may be unknown to the men running the roads; if it consists of government bonds whether he lives or dies is immaterial to the government, all his money is devoted to public uses just the same as if the government *confiscated* it and stopped interest on its bonds.

Not only is the principal of ten million dollars productively engaged, but $300,000 of the income goes back into productive uses.

Therefore *so long* as he continues to squander

only $200,000 per year, twenty-five thousand
dollars of which is not wasted, his economic
cost to the community is $175,000 per year; his
wealth of ten million dollars is a legal *fiction*.
It is very much as if the community gave him a
pension of $175,000 per year to squander.

❖   ❖   ❖

We have taken an extreme case. There are
many men and women, young and old, with
large incomes who spend viciously and foolishly large percentages of their incomes ; men
and women who are *veritable nuisances* to
themselves, their families, their cities — to
civilization itself.

But the number is not actually so large as is
commonly supposed; and with those the percentage of income absolutely wasted is not so
great as commonly reputed.

It is said that one swallow does not make a
summer, but it is pretty nearly true that one
fool makes a winter.

One monkey dinner, one dog luncheon,
heralded by the press, prejudices the entire
country not only against a large class, but
against a city.

The rich—the *richer*—man is everywhere, the rich farmer, merchant, manufacturer, banker.

And the overwhelming majority of rich men —of men who have more than the average— whether farmers or merchants, and whether worth ten thousand or ten millions *continue to work* in one way or another for the good of the community. If they "retire" from more active work it is to take up something else, some hobby, that may be of even greater benefit to the community.

IV

ONLY FOR LIFE

"We brought nothing into this world and it is certain we can carry nothing out."

So said Saint Paul and truly.

The rich man dies like the poor man, of all his wealth he takes not a penny with him.

At most therefore private property is but a life estate.

What a man does not actually consume during his lifetime he *must leave behind* for others to enjoy.

One moment he is said to be "worth" a million dollars, the next he breathes his last and is "worth" nothing.

The food we are eating may be said to be *our own* in the most absolute sense inasmuch as we are actually consuming and absorbing it.

The clothes we wear may be said to be our own, but in not quite so absolute a sense since our sudden death would leave them behind for others to use.

Others have a still greater reversionary interest in our houses, and so on.

The rich man spends a million dollars on a great estate in the country. He is said to " own " it, and so he does in a *legal* sense. The *law* — which is simply the custom of society as at present constituted — says he may have exclusive possession of the estate[1] during his lifetime, may sell it, lease it, dispose of it by will, and if he does not dispose of it by will the law names the heirs to whom the estate shall go on the " owner's " death, and if there are no heirs then the law says the estate shall go to the state, to the community, in which event the legal fiction of that particular private property vanishes in thin air.

In tribes it is the *custom,* and in civilized states it is the *law,* that on a man's death title to his property shall pass to certain persons, usually members of his family; if he leaves no family or relatives the tribe or the state may take his property, and the tribe or the state

---

[1] Always subject to the superior rights of the community such as the right of eminent domain, control for purposes of sanitation, etc., which need not here be enumerated but which very materially modify that absolute control which is popularly supposed to go with private property.

usually takes a portion as a matter of custom or under succession and inheritance tax laws.

Furthermore the *character* of the property makes a great difference in its disposition.

Every community recognizes the distinction between ownership of *realty* and *personalty*.

The land a man owns passes under certain special provisions of the law, while his personal property passes under separate and more or less different provisions.

In no two countries and in no two states of this country are the *succession laws* and inheritance taxes precisely the same, and in *every country* and *every state* these laws are undergoing changes *at the will of the community*.

For instance the laws of England and Scotland regarding the descent of *real* property are very different, and again in both countries the distribution of *personal property* is governed by entirely different regulations.

In England as regards *lands* the Rules of Inheritance apply, while as regards *personal* property the Statute of Distribution governs.

Until 1890 this last named statute provided

that where a man died without a will, leaving a widow and no children or next of kin, the widow took *one-half* the personal estate while the other half went to the Crown.

In the United States some of the states follow the Roman law, some the Common law, while others like California, Louisiana, and Texas follow French and Spanish law.

To add to the confusion it is generally the rule that the descent of real property is governed by the laws of the country or state where the property is situated, the distribution of personal property is governed by the laws of the country or state wherein the owner was domiciled—had his residence.

So that a man by buying a residence across a street, if that street happens to mark the line between two countries or states may without knowing it change materially the rights of his widow and relatives in the distribution of his personal estate, he may even limit his own power to dispose of that estate by will.

❖ ❖ ❖

The manner in which tribes from the most primitive states through to the most highly

civilized have treated *succession* to property
demonstrates clearly the purely *human* and
social character of all property rights, and the
community's *absolute control* over same.

❖ ❖ ❖

Now why have savage tribes by *custom* and
civilized states by *law* given certain persons,
family, and relatives, the right to *succeed* to—
that is *enter into possession* of —either all or a
portion of the dead man's property?

❖ ❖ ❖

First—for the obvious reason that when a
man *disappears,* or is *incapacitated by illness,*
or *dies, someone* must take possession of his
property.

If no parties are designated by custom or
law then there will be a *scramble* and the death
of each individual would be awaited—perhaps
accelerated—by all near at hand in order that
they might seize his possessions.

These conditions have actually prevailed in
whole or in part with the result that even
primitive tribes find it necessary to follow *customs* whereby either the chief, or the relatives

of the dead man, quietly assume possession of
his property.

❖ ❖ ❖

A *custom* or *law* of succession is necessary to
prevent *strife* and *waste*.

There is no question of *abstract right* involved.

A son has no more right to succeed to his
father's property than a daughter, or a brother,
or a cousin, or a stranger. *His* right is established by custom or law and may be curtailed
or abolished by custom or law.

It is so generally the custom for children and
near relatives to inherit that most people labor
under the impression they have a peculiar,
almost " sacred " right. It is highly important
to realize that no such abstract right exists.

❖ ❖ ❖

The foundation of the right of succession
and inheritance is *purely practical*.

True, the heirs or successors may prove
incompetent, but even at the risk, where there
is no will, of turning the property of the dead
man over to incompetent children or relatives,
experience has demonstrated it is wiser for the

community to have fixed laws of succession than it would be for the community to attempt to investigate in each instance the competency of the heirs and distribute the estate accordingly —a course *ideally* desirable but *practically* impossible.

The entire question of inheritance and succession is therefore a purely *economic question*.

The *sole object* of every inheritance or succession law should be to secure to the community the highest degree of efficiency in the management of the property *abandoned* by the man who has *disappeared, died,* or become incapacitated by illness or other causes.

❖ ❖ ❖

Whether existing inheritance and succession laws accomplish this object is a subject by itself.

The points we wish to impress here are;

Property is so *essentially* a community creation that individuals — poor and rich — come and go without lessening the wealth of the community by so much as a penny.

If Mr. Rockefeller should die tomorrow the wealth of the country and the world would not be increased or decreased by a single farthing. There would be a shifting of *titles* under the law, but that is all. And if it so happened the law could find no children or relatives to inherit and no will disposing of the estate, then the community would take it all.

We might put the matter this way; the community would first do all it could to find a *will* disposing of the estate; failing to find a will the community would then do all it could to find *relatives* to inherit; failing to find relatives the community would reluctantly take over the vast fortune and *try* to do the best it could with it.

Why do we say *"reluctantly,"* when most people would say the public would be mighty *glad* to get the fortune ?

We say *"reluctantly"* because that is the real *attitude* of the community toward succession generally. This is demonstrated by the fact that every community does provide by law that every effort shall be made to find *individuals* to take the property and manage it.

If experience of both tribes and civilized
peoples had not demonstrated that this is the
wiser *economic* course, communities long ago
would have established the custom of community succession.

As regards a given fortune the unthinking
portion of the public might be glad if no relatives could be found, but that would not be the
true and *logical* attitude of the community; the
feeling of satisfaction in the particular case
would be diametrically opposed to the spirit of
the inheritance laws.

Governments the world over are interfering
more and more with *private control* of property, to the extent of limiting and even abolishing it. On one pretext and another governments are appropriating, not to say confiscat-
ing, larger and larger percentages of estates
and possessions. From a stamp tax on a deed
to an inheritance or succession tax; from a succession tax to the appropriation of the entire
estate where there are no heirs and no will, it
is but a matter of degree in the assertion of the
superior rights of the community—the asser-

tion of the *real* ownership as against the *nominal*.

In Germany, even prior to the World War, the need of public revenue was so great that imperial right of succession (*Reichserbrecht*) was seriously advocated.

One form of the proposition was that first of all the tax on inheritance should be heavy; secondly that beyond brothers and sisters no collateral relations should inherit unless specifically provided for by will, but that all property now passing by law to such distant relations should pass to the state.

It was estimated[1] that this change in the laws of succession would yield the state over five hundred millions of marks.

If it did not yield sufficient revenue, obviously the next step along the same line would be for the state to take the place of brothers and sisters, or take one-half that goes to children, and so on to the taking of all a man leaves.

Granting the *power* and the *right* of the state

---

[1] Bernhardi, *Germany and the Next War*, pp. 269-271.

so to do, the *vital question* is the *economic expediency.*

Up to certain limits of appropriation by the state the individual might not be *discouraged.* Beyond certain limits the *incentive* to the individual to put forth his best efforts all his life long, would diminish.

❖   ❖   ❖

In the United States the powers of Congress and the various state legislatures to deal arbitrarily with property rights are limited by the federal and state constitutions.

The *constitutional restrictions* upon the powers of legislatures have led the American people to believe there is something *sacred* in property rights, something that is above and beyond the power of the community to do with it as it pleases.

There is nothing in this notion.

The community as a whole is all-powerful to regulate its internal affairs according to its best judgment.

This truth is recognized in the United States by *the power in the people to change their constitutions* as they please.

While the present constitutions stand, certain rights — such as certain property rights — are above the powers of legislatures to curtail. But in constitutional conventions the people can create and suppress rights to suit themselves. They can abolish constitutions and establish any form of socialism or communism they desire. They can limit the rights of the individual in any manner they deem best.

A man's *right* to what he has depends wholly upon the attitude of those about him. He has no right beyond social — i. e. commercial *recognition*. If the community wants what the individual has, it will take it away from him, and he will never think of asserting a *right* against the overwhelming voice of the community.

But if the community recognizes the fact that it is better for all that the individual's *dominion* be recognized within greater or lesser limits, *then* private property — i. e. private control — begins and is established.

For instance a man may " own " for miles the land on both sides of a navigable stream, but the community does not permit him to assert any ownership over the stream.

Again a man may " own " a large ranch and all the roads through it. The community develops to a point where it wants the roads so it appropriates them, and it may cut others and allow railroads to condemn rights of way, etc., etc.

Everybody recognizes the right of the community to pass the most stringent laws affecting personal liberty, affecting the right of the individual to *do* things; it goes without saying that the right of the community to pass laws affecting the right of the individual to *own* things is even clearer.

It is all a matter of *conduct* anyway. In one case it is a matter of our conduct with relation to *others;* in the other case it is a matter of our conduct with relation to *things.*

A dog " owns " a bone so long as he is strong enough or fleet enough to prevent other dogs from taking it.

Man " owns " a bone in a more highly developed sense because it has come to be the *sense,* the *custom,* and so the *law* of the community that it is to the *interest* of the community that the individual should not be compelled to fight to keep what he has fairly gotten.

It is even believed to be to the interest of the community in the long run that the possession of the individual should not be disturbed in many cases where he got control unfairly.

The community bars the rightful owner after a certain length of time by statutes of limitation, saying in effect, "Unless you claim your bone within reasonable time, you cannot disturb him who has it."

❖ ❖ ❖

In short the recognition of private property is nowhere absolute. It differs in every country.

Just now violent assaults are being made upon private ownership of large estates in countries so widely different as Russia, Great Britain, and Mexico.

From the land-owners go up cries of hardship, injustice, confiscation, robbery, etc., etc.

Whether any given proposition of appropriation or confiscation is *unfair* is a nice question and turns upon the extent to which a community by certain laws has encouraged the individual to do certain things, and then by sudden reversal of those laws deprived the individual of the fruits of his labors.

Precisely this sort of a question arises with every proposed reduction of a protective tariff, every proposed law prohibiting the manufacture or sale of alcoholic liquors, and in lesser degrees regarding the enforcement of pure food laws, etc.

A community develops along certain lines, under certain laws. Capital and labor are attracted to certain industries.

Suddenly the community experiences a change of heart, laws are passed that virtually destroy entire industries, possibly entire cities and sections.

There is no doubt about the *right,* the *power* of the community to do these things, the only question is one of *economic expediency* — will the proposed measures be beneficial to the entire community in the long run? If so then the so-called *right* of the individual must give way; or rather as *against* the welfare of the community the individual has no *rights.* His true rights will be found to coincide with the advancement of the whole.

❖ ❖ ❖

Those who believe in private property and defend it will make more headway if they frankly concede at the outset there is nothing *sacred* about it and that the community is *free* to do as it deems best with it — strengthen, modify, or totally abolish it.

Starting with those premises the discussion becomes *dispassionate* and scientific, the sole question being to what extent is the recognition of private rights over things necessary to the advancement of the community?

The world is getting restless; it challenges in a manner it never did before. It will not be silenced by a " Thou shalt not." It demands to know the reason why.

Men of property are becoming more liberal. True, the great, the overwhelming majority still accept their lands and their wealth — as the Kaiser accepted his throne — as if granted from on High, as possessions so peculiarly and sacredly their own that for others to interfere is sacrilegious. But there is a very intelligent

minority composed of men who would rather
think than make money, who would rather be
right than rich; this minority are also asking
the reason why — why and how private rights
over things have come to be what they are, and
whether as they are, they are essential to the
economic, intellectual, and spiritual advancement of the community, or whether on the
other hand some form of socialism or communism would not be better.

A great many teachers, professors, ministers, writers, are also asking the reason why.

The world is an animated interrogation
mark.

Not alone private property, but every social
and economic institution is under investigation.
Time-honored theories and explanations are
going by the board. Men will accept no man's
say-so. Authority is challenged. People are
bent upon getting to the root of things.

That is why the academic notions regarding
private property are having such a hard time.

That is why the land-owner, and the bondholder, and the stockholder are worrying.

They don't know what is about to happen. All they know is that the socialists are increasing in numbers, that communists and anarchists are found on every street corner, and the man with money is pointed out as a public enemy.

On first impression it would seem as if the cyclone cellar is the place for the unhappy millionaire, but that would be the flight of the coward and moreover he could not take his millions with him.

If ever the rich man needed to stand out in the open and justify his economic value he needs to now.

It is no time for dillydallying. If the people cannot be convinced that the rich man is at least as important and valuable a factor in the development of the community as the poor man then he will have to go.

It is not a question whether *he,* as an individual, has a *right* to his wealth; the sole question is whether it is a good thing for the community to permit him to exercise that right; whether the results in the long run are better than if the community took over in some way part or all of his rights.

It is precisely this very practical question that has not been fully and fairly considered and answered *because the true nature of private property* has not been fully understood.

It is always assumed that it is a question of the community on the one side with little or no control over the property, and the individual on the other with practically absolute powers of disposition.

If it were true that a man with a million or ten millions owned it in such a way that the community had little or no enjoyment thereof, then the argument for private property would be weak indeed — only the *sacred* theory would sustain it.

But if it should be found to be true that the individual " owning " a million virtually simply holds the *nominal title* for life, the *real enjoyment* of practically the entire fortune being in the community, then a very different aspect to the problem is presented, and it is this aspect that has not been discussed in the literature on the subject.

V

Russell Sage was famous in New York for his parsimony and his shrewdness. He lived very simply and devoted his entire time to loaning and investing his money.

Because he was not a lavish spender [1] and because he loaned and invested always with a view to getting the highest returns for his money, he was *not popular*.

Let us put it more directly, he was not popular because he was *thrifty* and *frugal* to a marked degree.

Curious, is it not?—that men who *spend* or *waste* wealth with reckless prodigality are usually popular, even though they go bankrupt and cause losses to thousands, while men who *save* and carefully invest productively are looked upon as " closefisted "—miserly—and are unpopular.

---

[1] When the elevated roads were first operated in New York the fare was ten cents except during the " rush " hours morning and evening. A friend who knew Sage says he often saw him standing in line waiting for the five-cent hour.

83

It is because people do not stop to think whose money is being wasted. The common impression is that the millionaire who spends extravagantly is simply wasting *his* wealth, that while he may go bankrupt others in the community get some benefit. Whereas the truth is that every dollar wasted is *community wealth,* the individual simply has the *power*— the legal " right "—to waste.

It does not matter whether the money is spent on ugly monuments, yachts, worthless pictures, fast horses, castles, dinners, balls, etc.; *every dollar* so spent is *community wealth.*

❖ ❖ ❖

Why, then, should a man like Russell Sage, who saves all his life be unpopular while another who recklessly spends the fortune he has made or inherited be popular?

The obvious answer is that the public does not understand the economic *worth* of the frugal man and the economic *worthlessness* of the foolish spender.

But there is another side — a curious psychological side. The public—like the Lord— " loveth a cheerful giver." From time immemorial people have thoughtlessly applauded the man who seemed to care so little about money he threw it right and left. His reckless freedom and generosity have obscured his economic and other sins.

❖   ❖   ❖

The attitude of the public toward spending will surely change as it begins to understand that the wealth wasted is *its* wealth, made by *it*, accumulated by *it*, though the recognition of certain property rights has given the individual the *power* to do with it as he pleases.

❖   ❖   ❖

From an economic point of view Russell Sage should have been *highly valued* by the people of New York, inasmuch as he was quietly, and at a *low cost* to the community, loaning, reloaning, and reinvesting many millions of money, and it was a matter of comment that he exercised more sagacity and foresight than almost any banker in the city.

He may have been " closefisted," " miserly," a hard man to deal with; he may have exacted a high rate of interest; may have called for his " pound of flesh " when due; but these are all economic traits, the traits of a *relentless trustee* of public funds.

He did not permit his sympathies or his imagination to swerve his business judgment. Seemingly his one aim in life was to keep every dollar he could get *productively* employed.

❖ ❖ ❖

While he was a rich man in the popular sense of the term he lived all his life as simply as many men working on fairly modest salaries.

His entire wealth was in the possession and control of others.

❖ ❖ ❖

He had no children. When he died in 1906 he left by will $650,000 to some twenty-nine relatives; the entire residue, over $60,000,000, he left to Mrs. Sage to do with as she pleased.

❖ ❖ ❖

His fortune when he died consisted of:
Cash — $612,619.

This represented, no doubt, his bank balances; money paid in faster than he could loan it out. But, if in bank, it would be productively engaged through bank loans.

Forty pieces of real estate — $1,945,500.

His investments in real estate were not large. It is worth noting in passing that his household furniture in his very unpretentious home, No. 632 Fifth Avenue, was appraised at only $8,052.

There were some twenty-three open accounts — money due him from various people; and fourteen mortgages.

The bulk of the estate consisted of some 152 loans to bankers, brokers, partnerships, corporations, individuals, etc. This was his specialty, loaning money to men in need of it, and the greater their need the greater his opportunity. He would often make loans at times and under conditions when banks hesitated. Naturally he would exact his compensation for the risk, and the very men benefited would often denounce him as a usurer. But because his fortune was " his own," that is to say because he was loaning " his own " money instead of the money of depositors he could take risks banks could not take, and it was an economic advantage to the community to have

Russell Sage's millions available in emergencies.

One has simply to look over the list of loans outstanding at the time of his death—loans ranging from $500,000 down—to appreciate the great variety of individuals, partnerships and companies he aided.

In addition to his loans he left stocks and bonds of over eighty steam and street railroads, and some sixty industrial companies; stocks in six banks; also city and state bonds.

He performed the functions of a bank except that instead of receiving deposits and loaning the money of others he had quite enough to do loaning and investing his own.

That he met an *economic need* and was a valuable *economic factor* in the development of the community was demonstrated by the price the community was glad to pay for his services.

He may have had personal characteristics which made him unpopular, but for that matter most banks are not popular institutions—that is there is a popular feeling against bankers as compared with merchants and manufacturers.

In the popular mind the manufacturer is looked upon as a *producer* like the farmer; the merchant is looked upon as a necessary and useful factor in *distribution;* but the popular mind fails to grasp the economic importance of the banker because it looks as if he simply juggled with money, producing nothing, distributing nothing.

The thinking man knows the banker performs just as useful services as the manufacturer or the merchant; the banker is an economic necessity in order that the farmer, the manufacturer, the merchant may develop and make the most of his opportunities.

As we approach the utopia the need for bankers and money-loaners as we know them may lessen, but if so it will be because of some more scientific and economical method of performing the services they now perform.

One thing is certain the economic utopia will be attained — if ever — only along the lines of increasing mobility of wealth. Economic progress is in direct ratio to the *ductility* of wealth, to the safety, ease, and rapidity with which it flows from point to point, from enterprise to enterprise. At present this ductility depends almost entirely upon the services of bankers and of individuals, like Sage, who perform services akin to those of bankers.

❖ ❖ ❖

What happened after his death?

The fortune was steadily withdrawn from productive uses and devoted to charitable and philanthropic purposes.

Naturally Mrs. Sage had neither the desire nor the ability to go on investing and reinvesting in order to accumulate more. That is a man's work.

Her interests and inclination were in other directions, in the direction of *distribution* rather than accumulation.

It is as if he and she had formed a life partnership wherein it was agreed that he should devote all his life to accumulation, and on his death she should undertake the far more difficult task of distribution. He took the hard, *economic, unpopular* work, leaving to her the generous, philanthropic, popular task.

Each may be a valuable factor in the life and development of the community.

But the *risk* to the community began *after* his death, when the work of *withdrawing* and *spending* the fortune began.

❖ ❖ ❖

During his lifetime he had only pieces of paper, his fortune was a *potentiality,* it did not exist except on paper.

After his death the fortune began to *emerge,* so to speak, to materialize as piece after piece of paper was disposed of, as interest and dividends were held and spent instead of being reinvested productively.

Much of the fortune still exists *in paper,* is still engaged productively, but year by year Mrs. Sage drew out large amounts and spent the same for philanthropic and public objects.

So far as the community is concerned it is as if the state had inherited the fortune and was steadily devoting it to the same uses, only the *cost* of distribution is very different.

The *cost* to the community of distributing the Sage fortune — up to the date of Mrs. Sage's death — was what Mrs. Sage spent on herself and what she paid her advisers — probably not a large amount all told.

If the state had inherited the fortune, every-one knows that a large portion of it would have been wastefully used in the support of offices and office-holders.

The public would rather leave the distribution of these millions to a woman and her trusted advisers, people whose sole thought is to do all the good they can, than leave it to either the State House in Albany or the City Hall in New York.

Mrs. Sage and her advisers may have made mistakes, but they were honest mistakes of heart and judgment. They did not plunder the estate or spend a dollar for political advantages.

❖   ❖   ❖

One of the greatest defects of our governing and administrative mechanism is that the community has practically no *machinery* for the spending of money except *political*.

It is a common knowledge that a man may be a very good legislator and a very poor business man or philanthropist.

It is a fatal defect so far as efficiency and disinterestedness are concerned to permit Con-

gress or any *legislative* body to have anything
to do with the manner in which money shall be
spent by the spending departments.

A business department such as the post office
should not have its headquarters at Washington. The gross impropriety of the railroads
of the country maintaining headquarters in
Washington has been demonstrated, yet if the
government bought the railroads the headquarters would be at once established within
the shadow of the capitol [1] with the inevitable
result, the railroads would become a part of
the huge *political* machine.

We are beginning to see why all advanced
people *instinctively* uphold property rights and
extend them after the death of the individual.

First of all it is because fortunes that exist
on paper are in reality *more efficiently* engaged
in production than if the community had the
title.

Secondly, when those who have accumulated
or inherited the fortunes begin spending and
giving, *as a rule* they do it with less waste and
less cost, and with *finer foresight and imagina-*

---

[1] As has been the case during the war.

tion than if the community seized and spent the fortunes.

❖ ❖ ❖

Mrs. Sage died November 4, 1918, leaving a will which made a final distribution of the Sage fortune.

During the twelve years she survived her husband she gave away between thirty and forty millions of dollars, in part as follows:

FOR CHARITABLE INSTITUTIONS

An endowment fund of $10,000,000 to the Russell Sage Foundation, the income to be used for the betterment of social and living conditions.

To the Russell Sage Institute of Pathology, an endowment fund of $300,000.

For the Association for Relief of Respectable, Aged, Indigent Females, an addition to its building on 104th Street, $25,000.

Adirondack Cottage Sanitarium, $25,000.

Working Girls' Home on East Twelfth Street, $25,000.

To the Young Men's Christian Association, for a new building for the International Committee, on Twenty-eighth Street, New York, $350,000.

For addition to Y. M. C. A. Building at Brooklyn Navy Yard, about $340,000. For building at Fort McKinley, Philippines, $25,-000; for Long Island Railroad Branch, new building at Long Island City, $100,000; for new building at Fort Slocum, $50,000.

EDUCATIONAL INSTITUTIONS

Rensselaer Polytechnic Institute, Troy, $1,-000,000.

Troy Female Seminary, (Emma Willard School), $1,000,000.

Harvard University, a new dormitory.

Yale University, the Hillhouse property, consisting of thirty acres, at a cost of about $650,000. This constitutes what is now known as the Pierson-Sage Campus.

Princeton University, dormitories and tower. New York University, for the purchase of additional land about $300,000.

Northfield Seminary, a memorial chapel.

Gifts to Syracuse University, Idaho Industrial Institute, Lincoln University, Girls' School at Constantinople, and the Berry School at Rome, Georgia.

To the Metropolitan Museum of Art, the Bolles Collection of American Colonial furniture and household art.

FOR NATIONAL OR CITY PURPOSES

Constitution Island, opposite West Point, purchased and presented to the United States Government.

The City Hall in New York, as respects the rotunda and the governor's room, restored under the direction of the Art Commission.

Large plantations of rhododendrons, at a cost of about $60,000, for Central Park.

Libraries of technical books to each of the 258 fire houses in New York City.

For Sag Harbor, Long Island, a public library, including land, building, books, and endowment, a new public school, and an extensive playground.

A bird refuge in southern Louisiana, known as Marsh Island, consisting of about 70,000 acres.

By her will she distributed the balance of the estate. Aside from a bequest of eight millions to her brother and other personal bequests amounting to about two hundred thousand dollars the entire fortune then in her hands, estimated at over forty millions, was given away.

On the face of the will the residue would be distributed approximately as follows:

Russell Sage Foundation........$5,600,000
Troy Female Seminary.......... 1,600,000
Woman's Hospital in the State of
New York 1,600,000
Board of Home Missions of the
Presbyterian Church of America
(Woman's Executive Committee). 1,600,000

Woman's Board of Foreign Missions of the Presbyterian Church. 1,600,000

New York City Mission and Tract Society 1,600,000

American Bible Society.......... 1,200,000

New York Bible Society.......... 400,000

Children's Aid Society........... 1,600,000

Charity Organization Society..... 1,600,000

Presbyterian Board of Relief for Disabled Ministers and the Widows and Orphans of Deceased Ministers 800,000

Metropolitan Museum of Art..... 1,600,000

American Museum of Natural History 1,600,000

New York Botanical Garden..... 800,000

New York Zoological Society...... 800,000

New York Public Library........ 800,000

Troy Polytechnic Institute........ 800,000

Union College, Schenectady....... 800,000

Syracuse University 1,600,000

Hamilton College, Clinton, N. Y... 800,000

New York University............ 800,000

Yale University................. 800,000

Amherst College 800,000

Williams College 800,000

Dartmouth College 800,000

Princeton University 800,000

Barnard College 800,000

Bryn Mawr College............. 800,000

Vassar College 800,000

Smith College 800,000

Wellesley College 800,000

Tuskegee Normal and Industrial Institute 800,000

New York Infirmary for Women
and Children 800,000
Presbyterian Hospital in the City
of New York..................... 800,000
State Charities Aid Association... 800,000
Hampton Institute 800,000
Troy Female Seminary.......... 50,000
Association for the Relief of Re-
spectable, Aged, Indigent Females
in the City of New York.......... 125,000
Woman's Hospital in the State of
New York 50,000
Board of Home Missions of the
Presbyterian Church of the United
States of America (Woman's Ex-
ecutive Committee of Home Mis-
sions) 25,000
Woman's Board of Foreign Mis-
sions of the Presbyterian Church.. 25,000
New York City Mission and Tract
Society (Woman's Board)........ 20,000
New York Female Auxiliary Bible
Society 10,000
Children's Aid Society of the City
of New York.................... 10,000
Charity Organization Society of
the City of New York............ 20,000
First Presbyterian Church of Syra-
cuse 10,000
First Presbyterian Church of Sag
Harbor 10,000
Society for the Relief of Half-Or-
phan and Destitute Children of the
City of New York............... 25,000

New York Institute for the Deaf and Dumb	25,000
Home for the Friendless..........	100,000
New York Exchange for Women's Work	25,000
Woman's National Sabbath Alliance	25,000
Ladies' Christian Union of the City of New York	100,000
Working Women's Protective Union	10,000
Servants of Relief for Incurable Cancer	25,000
Salvation Army	25,000
Park College	100,000
Idaho Industrial Institute........	200,000
Old Ladies' Home at Syracuse....	25,000
Northfield Schools (Northfield Seminary and Mount Hermon Boys' School)	100,000
Middlebury College	100,000
Rutgers College	100,000
Y. M. C. A. of the City of New York	100,000
Y. W. C. A. of the City of New York	100,000
Mount Sinai Hospital............	100,000
Syracuse University	100,000
Hampton Institute	100,000

In the twelve years since the death of Russell Sage the benefactions of Mrs. Sage reached a total estimated to be between $35,000,000 and $40,000,000, so that, during her life and after her death, her gifts for public uses make up a sum between $75,000,000 and $80,000,000. The philanthropies of John D. Rockefeller and Andrew Carnegie are the only ones believed to have been greater.

Mrs. Sage had used a part of the capital as well as the income of the estate for her philanthropies, so that the property she leaves is less by several millions than that which was left to her. She received from her husband's estate $64,153,800.91.

The first and obvious comment is that a woman of ninety could not possibly have ascertained the needs of all the institutions and objects named.

She was guided by either her mere impulses or by her advisers. If by her advisers then they and not she distributed the fortune and as they are not named publicly and assume no responsibility the net result is the arbitrary withdrawal of millions from productive employment and the distribution of same by men —her advisers—who are not named and not called upon to justify their judgment.

No doubt the institutions and objects named

will make good use of the bequests and to the
extent they do, the money may be productive of
social good in a finer sense than if left in com-
merce and industries.

The thought we have in mind here is the
chance the community runs when it permits and
even encourages elderly individuals to arbitrarily transfer their fortunes from investments — productive employment — to a long
list of objects, the needs of which cannot be
accurately ascertained by them.

The community may be immensely benefited
by the foresight, the imagination, the constructive genius of the giver; *per contra* it *may* be
economically injured by the folly, the egotism,
the ignorance of the giver.

❖   ❖   ❖

The following editorial from a leading New
York daily is a fair sample of the press com-
ments on the final distribution of the Sage
fortune:

It would be difficult to dispose of a great estate
more sagaciously and justly than Mrs. Russell Sage
has done by her will. She leaves some forty millions
for educational, philanthropic and charitable purposes. Colleges, libraries, hospitals, the Metropolitan

Museum of Art and the American Museum of Natural
History, the Children's Aid Society, the Charity Organization Society, the Infirmary for Women and
Children, and many other institutions are splendidly
remembered.   There are specific legacies to many organizations.   To name only Mount Sinai Hospital,
Hampton Institute, the Salvation Army, the Working
Woman's Protective Union, the New York Institution
for the Deaf and Dumb, the Home for the Friendless,
is to illustrate faintly the scope of Mrs. Sage's benefactions.   The most cynical social sorehead and
growler at philanthropy will be pleased by her re-
membrance of her old servants.

In the twelve years from the time of Mr. Sage's
death Mrs. Sage gave for public uses between thirty-
five and forty millions.   By will she has given away
forty millions more.   *The greater part of the fortune
accumulated by Mr. Sage has been returned to the
public.*   It is the fashion for light-brained, envious
folk, amateur socialists or budding Bolsheviki, to
abuse "wealth" and gnash their teeth at "the rich."
*Yet how swiftly the great fortunes melt; in a genera-
tion or two they generally come back to the public.*
It took only twelve years to scatter most of Mr.
Sage's, or, rather, to invest it forever in trust for good
objects.   As a rule the Americans who get notably
rich make the people their heir.

This sort of praise is both thoughtless and
mischievous.

Attention is called especially to the idea
conveyed in the lines *italicized* by the writer,

the statement the fortune has at last *"been returned to the public,"* as if in some manner — by inference more or less reprehensible — the public had been deprived of the fortune during Sage's lifetime.

Almost *precisely the reverse* was true.

It was during the *accumulation* of the fortune that the public enjoyed full possession and use, and if Russell Sage the day before his death had burned every note, every bond, every share of stocks, every account-book — in short every piece of paper evidencing his legal title to his fortune so that no one, not even the state, could trace and draw out a dollar of his fortune, the public would have been far more materially served than by the attempts made to draw out from productive uses his millions and devote them to educational, philanthropic, and charitable uses.

The question of ultimate value to society would depend upon the balance that would have to be struck between the value of a fortune of sixty or eighty millions continuing undisturbed in industrial, commercial, banking, railroading, and other productive pursuits, and the value of the same fortune withdrawn and devoted to educational, charitable, and philanthropic purposes.

Such a balance can never be struck in figures. The wise and far-seeing expenditure of a million dollars in some commercially unproductive manner, such as the founding of a library, a school, an art museum, a settlement house, and so on, may be of incomparably greater value spiritually, aesthetically, socially, and ultimately economically, than leaving the million in a steel plant or a railroad. Everything depends upon the wisdom and, above all, the fine *imagination* of the giver.

The point here is that *before the giving begins* the fortune is *unquestionably* in the possession of the public, and not a dollar can be given away except the dollar is first taken from those using it productively. Whether the public ever again gets the benefit of the dollar depends upon the wisdom of the donor and the social necessity of the object, philanthropic or otherwise, to which the money is devoted.

Mrs. Sage was seventy-eight when her husband died. She was ninety when she died. Generally speaking men and women between eighty and ninety are not capable physically or mentally of suddenly undertaking the *giving away* of large amounts of money.

Even if they are mentally quite vigorous they lack the physical strength to make the proper inquiries and investigations, and critically follow results.

Therefore, generally speaking, laws and institutions which give the extremely aged such powers call for critical comment to say the least, and indiscriminate praise of such giving as a "return to the public," is based on a fundamental misconception.

These conclusions are so diametrically opposed to popular impression they will bear restating.

❖ ❖ ❖

So long as a man is industriously engaged in *accumulating* his fortune by fair and honorable means the community is a *gainer*, because by his productive efforts he is steadily adding to the sum total of *actual* wealth, while at the

same time he is increasing his *nominal* wealth
— i. e., his *legal right* to *withdraw* and divert
some to other uses when he pleases.

So long as the fortune of an individual is *left
in* a business, the *economic effect* from year to
year is precisely as if the community owned
the fortune. The community gets the services
of the individual *at the cost* of what he draws
out for living and other personal expenditures.

The danger of loss and interruption of productive processes begins when the individual
begins to *assert his ownership* — when he
begins to withdraw his fortune and devote it to
other purposes.

And the danger lies in the possibility he will
spend it or *give it away* in such a manner that
it will do the community less good than if the
money were left in the particular business or
industry.

The general impression is that while a man
is *accumulating* he is engaged in a purely

selfish pursuit, and that when he stops accumulating and begins distributing he is engaged in a *nobly unselfish pursuit.*

❖ ❖ ❖

In a profound sense the *reverse* is true.

The term "selfish" is much abused. It suffers a largely undeserved odium.

In a fine sense everything we do that is worth doing is done from purely selfish motives.

When we start out to do things *professedly* for the benefit of others, we usually make a failure unless at the same time we *gratify ourselves* in a high degree, and the greater the benefit to others—the more *seemingly* unselfish our conduct—the more noble the self-gratification; if *not* then there is something wrong with our conduct.

The most *unselfish* act the mind of man could devise would be at the same time the most *purely* selfish.

❖ ❖ ❖

The very foundation of faith, hope, charity, love, is selfishness—interest in the gratification, the development, the future, of one's own self.

The familiar test of everyday life is whether a man in what he does thinks *first* of himself and secondly or remotely of others; or whether he *forgets* himself in his efforts to do things that benefit others.

Judged by these tests it is quite apparent a man not only *may,* but *usually does,* forget himself more when he is absorbed in his work of building up a business or industry; often forgets himself to the undermining of his health and the sacrifice of his life.

When it comes to *giving away* his money a man rarely forgets himself. Few men sacrifice either their lives or their comfort in the service of charity or philanthropy.

So far from forgetting themselves men generally court publicity — love to see their names in print and on buildings and monuments — the really selfish — in an objectionable sense — period of their lives begins.

When a man begins to *spend* his fortune the community is vitally interested in the question: Is he spending or giving *wisely* or *foolishly,*

not from his individual point of view, but from the community's ?

❖ ❖ ❖

The *accumulation* of wealth is one thing, its consumption is quite different.

As a factor in accumulating, a man may be a most valuable citizen. As a *director* of distribution and consumption he may be a costly failure.

During the better part of his life he may be *productively* engaged in adding to the total wealth of the community, as well as in increasing his own fortune.

During the latter portion of his life he may be *destructively* engaged in withdrawing his fortune from the productive wealth of the community and using that fortune in ways that do the community little or no good.

On the other hand he may be *constructively* engaged in performing an invaluable service in devoting his fortune to works and objects of practical, scientific, aesthetic value which would not be created or encouraged were it not for his taste, his foresight, his imagination, his ambition to do something of great and lasting good.

The value of the rich man to the community may be twofold;

1. As a *producer* and an *accumulator*.
2. As a *distributor*.

As a producer he is so valuable an *economic factor* that every community that has attained any degree of advancement has found it a *good, practical, business proposition* to permit men to retain for themselves large control over what they produce as an *incentive* to work harder.

A man may *call* the wealth he is producing "his own." The community instinctively knows that *both he* and his *wealth* belong to the community.

As a distributor of his wealth the rich man may prove of even greater value to the community than as a producer.

As a producer he may be simply one of thousands equally industrious and equally efficient.

As a distributor he may display both *genius* and *imagination*.

He may do things for the public that the public would not do for itself for generations.

He may endow educational institutions, establish scientific research bodies, build art galleries, museums, libraries; he may support orchestras, theaters, enrich hospitals — all with the same *executive ability* that marked the accumulation of his wealth.

And all these things he may do long before any city or state would do them, and do them incomparably more brilliantly and efficiently.

❖ ❖ ❖

In the matter of investment and reinvestment the individual performs an economic service that cannot be done as well by public bodies, chiefly for the reason the individual *delights in taking risks* no public body is permitted to take.

❖ ❖ ❖

The speculative element is strong in man. The *sure* thing does not appeal to the man of imagination. The love of danger, of *risk,* is deeply implanted in human nature.

Investing one's money in safe " gilt-edged "

bonds is a cold-blooded proposition that arouses
no large degree of enthusiasm. Accumulating
wealth in that fashion is a deadly proposition;
it withers the soul. The man who does it is a
valuable economic factor, but he is like a timid
banker who loans only on gilt-edged collateral
—of no use when it comes to financing some
business or enterprise the outcome of which is
doubtful, but which, if successful, will be of
great benefit to the community. The great
banker takes chances on the *personality* of his
borrower, on the *human equation.*

The great rich man in reinvesting his money
instinctively loves to take chances not only on
men but on the *future of the country;* he takes
long chances in the construction of railways
into uninhabited territory because he believes
the people will follow and *some day* the roads
will pay; and if he never gets his money back
he will have had the satisfaction of attempting
a big thing for the country.

He builds waterworks, gasworks, electric-
light and power plants, street-car lines, *long
before* the towns would build them. He puts
his money into them freely, recklessly. In

endeavoring to get his money out, to make a profit, the companies he organizes may do things that exasperate the public, but it must never be forgotten that nearly all of these public works are *started* by men who would have *accumulated* wealth faster by investing in surer things!

Because here and there unprincipled men make millions out of public enterprises by methods that are corrupt and criminal does not alter the fact that *individual initiative* is back of practically every great work, big and little.

Individual initiative built the Suez Canal; individual initiative started the Panama Canal.

Into these and other public enterprises rich men and poor men pour their savings like water — why?

Because the investments are safe? Not at all. Rather because they are *unsafe,* because there is a *vague* promise of large profits in return for the great risks.

Appeal to the rich man — to any man, for that matter — through his *imagination* and he is the most gullible person on earth.

Whether it is in founding an orchestra, erect-

ing a library, establishing an art museum, or
building a railroad, the enthusiasm that enables
him to carry the work to completion depends
upon the strength of the appeal to his imagination.

Without knowing it many of our rich men
after working hard for years to accumulate
their wealth turn *poets* and *dreamers* in spending it, and because they are poets and dreamers
they inspire others, even carry the entire public with them, often to the attempting of something beyond the strength of both themselves
and the public. Just as De Lesseps, the poet
and dreamer, rather than De Lesseps, the
engineer, carried the French public off its feet
in the disastrous attempt to build the Panama
Canal.

A rich man who has gained his wealth by
corruption and who is unscrupulous in his
methods may also be a poet and a dreamer in
his enterprises; he may spend his wealth in
ways that almost make the public forget and
forgive the manner of its accumulation.

The facts and arguments, pro and con, con-
tained in this chapter indicate one conclusion

which should be more clearly outlined, and that is;

It is the *spending* of a fortune that calls for supervision.

A fortune is *accumulated* by investing and reinvesting, by keeping it at all times productively employed *in the hands of others*. The man who " owns " the fortune may confine his activities to a small desk in a small office. As the years go by the pieces of paper in his safety-vault box increase in number. As a matter of fact he does not control or in any way attempt to interfere with the way the properties represented by those pieces of paper are used, the men running the properties probably do not know of his existence.

So long as he lives the life of a careful and shrewd investor the community is beyond question a gainer by his judgment.

But when at seventy or eighty, or by will, he takes it into his head to realize on his pieces of paper and *spend* his fortune, the community *should become immediately and vitally interested*.

And possibly this interest should extend to

some sort of supervision of the transfer of
millions from unquestionably productive uses
to uses that may be either far more or far less
productive.

In other words should an old man be permitted to spend " his " fortune capriciously, or
take it to a foreign country—in short to do
" as he pleases " with it ?

The fortune while nominally and legally
" his " is so fundamentally the property of the
community where it is productively employed
that the " right " of the individual to do what
he wills with it, regardless of consequences, is
a " right " that calls for consideration and possibly some curtailment of a supervisory character—curtailment that will permit a wide
play to the individual imagination, insight, and
foresight, but at the same time secure the community against the waste that so often attends
mere giving—indiscriminate giving.

Perhaps the supervision cannot be exercised
without depriving the community of precisely
those benefits that result from the individual's
impulsive and arbitrary indulgence of his
dreams, his aspirations, his beliefs, and in the

long run it may be better for the community to go along as it does and take the chance referred to, but the subject of supervision is suggested —not advocated—because it must occur to every man who gives the matter serious thought.

VI

The late Marshall Field of Chicago started life in a New England town with nothing.

He became the greatest dry-goods merchant the world has known, and died leaving a fortune officially inventoried as follows:

Personal property $58,473,292.55
Real estate 24,985,739.83
_____

Total $83,459,032.38

The real estate consisted of:

His home on Prairie Avenue in the city of Chicago, occupying a frontage of 163 feet and improved with a three-story dwelling-house, so quiet and modest in appearance the entire place is hardly distinguishable from that of hundreds of men of moderate means.

Lots and parcels of land in many different states, some improved, others unimproved; also some farm lands, and some contracts for the purchase of real estate.

With the exception of his home all these

items of *real estate,* amounting to twenty-five millions of dollars, were *investments for profit,* investments made with the expectation that *advancing values* in the different neighborhoods would yield him a profit, even though he did nothing but hold the pieces and pay taxes on them.

This sort of *investment* is *fundamentally different* from investments in productive enterprises, and stress is here laid upon the *real* estate part of the Field fortune because *fortunes in real estate* will be discussed farther on.

For the moment we are interested in the *personal* property he accumulated.

The official inventory showed only $58,473,-292.55, but in this inventory all stocks and bonds were taken at *par* — at *face value.*

Stocks that had a *market* — an actual — value of $200 or $300 per share were inventoried at their par value of $100. [1]

---

[1] It must be understood there was nothing illegal or improper in so doing. In making an inventory it is quite correct to list stocks, bonds, notes, etc., and all pieces of property by their *description.* The *official appraisers* take the inventory and *appraise* the actual value regardless of the par or nominal value.

For instance he held 34,000 shares of the stock of Marshall Field & Co.—the greatest mercantile firm in the world—and these were taken in the inventory at their par, $100 per share, a nominal total for his controlling interest in that great business, of only $3,400,000.

No one can estimate the actual value of his interest in that very profitable business, but it would be nearer $50,000,000 than $3,000,000. [1] His fortune was probably not less than $150,-000,000.

❖ ❖ ❖

In addition to his interest in Marshall Field & Co., Mr. Field left the following items:

Money *in box,* $4,134.90.

Special attention is directed to this item for —aside from his home and personal belongings—it represents practically his *entire wealth* in *possession.* [2]

He had less than five thousand dollars in cash

---

[1] The par value of Mr. Carnegie's stock in the Carnegie Steel Company was $100 per share. He received for it $1,500 per share.

[2] Even then only in so far as the money was in gold — probably not a dollar. For paper money is simply promises to pay, notes.

idle. And the astonishing thing is that he had
so much. He was not a man to keep a penny
idle. Sudden sickness and death (from pneu-
monia, away from home) probably caught him
before this cash could be deposited in bank or
invested.

Money on deposit in various banks — $4,295,-
378.76.

This represents the current accumulation of
profits and interest from all his investments.
Naturally as money poured in from his business and from various investments he would
deposit it in different banks, and invest it as
fast as he could in many different ways — as
shown by the inventory of his estate.

Money in bank is *not idle.* As already noted
a bank is but a mechanism for keeping the
money of individuals *invested productively.* It
takes your money and mine, keeps a small percentage *on hand* to honor our checks, and *loans*
the balance to mechanics, farmers, manufacturers, business men — to anybody who needs
money and whose credit or security is good.

Deposited in bank Marshall Field's $4,000,-
000 were placed where the community could use

them by paying to the banks the current rate of interest, which interest the banks would divide with Marshall Field by allowing him probably two per cent on his daily balance.

Inasmuch as he could get only two per cent on his daily bank balances the *incentive* was always *strong* to get the money out of the banks and into stocks and bonds or other investments that would yield more, and that is what he did.

He not only ran—*personally supervised and built up*—his great mercantile business until it was literally one of the *commercial wonders* of this great commercial country, but he also exercised his keen judgment in investing his profits.

He would pour all he could back into his own business, then invest the surplus wherever it seemed most needed.

The official inventory showed the following items:

Stocks of 23 railroads.........$8,993,600.00
Stocks in 5 street railroads.....   194,700.00
Stocks in 17 banks.............   781,760.00

Stocks in 27 industrial and miscellaneous companies 7,001,950.00
Bonds of 30 railroads.......... 5,659,500.00
Bonds of 9 industrial and miscellaneous companies 1,903,500.00
Subscriptions to various enterprises 1,835,470.00
Notes of industrial companies and others 2,207,971.26
Money loaned Marshall Field & Co......................... 8,486,607.23

It is the *character* of a man's investments, not their *amount,* which determines his *economic* value to the community.

Whether the *market* value of any particular stock is above or below par does not alter the fact that the investment was made for *productive* purposes.

The market value—i. e. the price—of the stock, on any given day is an index of the *opinion* of the market regarding the productivity—the earning power—of the industry, and that may be large one year and small the next, or it may fail entirely, thereby discrediting the judgment of the men who invested in it.

At the time of his death the great majority of Mr. Field's stocks and bonds were above par, and worth more than when he invested, thereby demonstrating his *economic value* as a factor in wisely distributing his (the community's) wealth where it was most needed for productive purposes.

❖   ❖   ❖

The *net result* to the community of his life, from a purely economic view, was:

1. The devotion of exceptional executive genius to the development and organization of a great mercantile business, which not only served the public well, but also served as a model for similar establishments the world over. What he did for the country in advancing the *science*—the *art* if you please —of merchandising can hardly be overestimated in dollars and cents. So perfect and advanced in methods was his organization that in effect it was akin to a revolutionizing invention.

The great, the enterprising, the original business man, manufacturer, lawyer, doctor, is as much an *inventor* as the man who takes out patents on his ideas.

In fact the successful man in any walk of life must be an *originator,* an *inventor,* throughout his active career, and his success is measured by his originality, his daring, his innovations.

2. In addition to his executive ability as a great merchant the community had the benefit of Mr. Field's keenness of judgment in investing his earnings. He not only *invested* his money in railroads, banks, industries, etc., but he gave of his *time* and *energies;* he served as director with many companies, and his service was never perfunctory. He was not a "straw director."

❖ ❖ ❖

Now, what did all this cost the community up to the time of his death?

The comparatively *small amount* he spent on himself. His home was very unpretentious, and he lived so simply and inexpensively it was a matter of comment by those who knew him best.

Look at it this way, take every dollar he spent on himself and for his family, *double that amount,* would not the city of Chicago say the total was a small amount to pay for the development of the one mercantile enterprise, Marshall Field & Co.?

Is it *conceivable* that at so low a cost any commission, or any *socialistic community* could develop so successful and *economically valuable* an establishment?

The growth of this great business from small beginnings is one proof of the *economic value* of the liberal recognition of *personal property rights*.

Without such recognition as an *incentive* no man would work *all his life accumulating*. Why should he accumulate if his control, his authority over the accumulations are denied? His efforts would naturally and inevitably cease at the point where his control ceased. He would consume what he earned from year to year. He would not deny himself a single luxury for the sake of dying and leaving a fortune to the state.

His fortune *may* go to the state if he leaves no relatives and no will, but that possibility does not trouble him for every man expects to leave at least a will, and whether he does or not he labors on that assumption.

The item in the inventory: " Syndicate subscriptions — $1,835,470.00 " leads to an explana-
tion how men both rich and poor invest their
profits, incomes and savings in *productive*
enterprises.

Take an enterprise *already established* which
needs money for further development. It may
be a railroad, a coal-mining company, a lumber
company, a packing-house, or any other industry.

An estimate is made of the amount of money
needed and the company proposes to issue
stocks, or bonds, or both for the amount.

On first impression the simplest and easiest
way would seem to be to offer the securities to
the public generally, but up to the present time
that has not been found the practical and
expeditious way in this country, for the reason
the public generally has no knowledge of the
particular industry and no means of forming
an estimate of the value of the securities
offered, and there would be few or no subscribers.

Sometimes issues of bonds or new stock are
quickly subscribed by stockholders of the com-

pany because they know the earning power of
the company and have confidence in its future,
but the public can know very little about a new
enterprise.

Hence it is common practice for the men
engaged in an industry that needs more money,
or who are organizing a new enterprise, such
as a street railway, waterworks, electric-light
company, etc., etc., to formulate their plans and
lay them before bankers and other experts.

If the bankers and experts are favorably
impressed with the plans, they organize a
syndicate to subscribe for *all* of the new securities, and each member of the syndicate, whether
a bank or an individual, signs for the amount
opposite his name — just as Mr. Field subscribed for certain amounts in the syndicates
referred to. This *insures* the furnishing of the
money.

After the syndicate subscription is filled the
next step is to offer the securities to the public.
If the public, as often happens, subscribes for
the entire issue then the syndicate members
get no securities at all on their syndicate
subscriptions.

But if the public, as also often happens, takes only a part of the securities, then the unsold balance must be taken by the syndicate members, distributed in proportion to their subscriptions.

A syndicate agreement is, therefore, a *guaranty* to the new — or old — enterprise that the money it needs will surely be forthcoming at a given date whether or not the public takes any stock or bonds.

This guaranty is of value because it enables the men engaged in the industry to go ahead with their plans without waiting the slow and uncertain outcome of a popular subscription.

The syndicate has — or rather *should* have — another value; it signifies to the public that experts have looked into the enterprise and reported favorably, otherwise bankers and keen business men would not take the risk of guaranteeing the new capital.

For this service — this insurance — the syndicate usually receives a commission. If the public takes *all* the new securities then the members of the syndicate are relieved of their guaranty, they get no stocks or bonds, but they get as compensation the commission agreed upon.

The fact that many syndicate transactions and commissions have been of a character to call for condemnation, does not alter the truth that *generally speaking* the syndicate method of raising new capital is not only useful, but seemingly necessary in many cases.

Another and very common way of securing new capital is for the individual or corporation to sell its bonds direct to one or more banks or trust companies, which, in turn, sell them to their depositors and customers.

Banks and trust companies do not buy bonds with the expectation of *holding* them, but with the expectation of selling them at a profit, so as to be able to repeat the transaction.

It is plain that it makes little difference to either the company issuing the bonds or to the public that ultimately gets them for investment, whether a *syndicate subscribes* for them or a *bank buys* them. As a matter of fair calculation the profit of the bank that *buys outright* ought to be a little higher than that of the syndicate which only *guarantees,* and in the end may not be called upon to take any.

The syndicate method of securing capital *ought* to be less expensive.

❖ ❖ ❖

From the foregoing explanation it is plain that the signing of a syndicate subscription *involves no immediate* investment or expenditure.

No member of a syndicate invests or puts up a dollar until called upon by the syndicate managers, and if the public takes the entire issue of securities the syndicate members receive their commission and are released without the investment of a penny.

Herein is where men of wealth — like banks — perform a valuable economic service.

Their *credit* is such that their *mere agreement* to do certain things is accepted and serves the same purpose as if they actually deposited gold with their subscriptions.

Suppose it were necessary for syndicate subscribers to put up in gold the full amounts of their subscriptions, that would mean the *withdrawing* of so much money from productive uses, and holding it *idle* in vaults until the transaction was brought to a conclusion. It would make the raising of new capital more difficult and therefore more expensive. The result would be a *checking* of industrial and commercial development, a positive burden on the prosperity of the country.

❖ ❖ ❖

The fact that there are banks, trust companies, insurance companies, etc., and also large numbers of individuals whose credit is such that their mere *agreement* takes the place and for a time performs the work of *actual* wealth, *means much* in the economic development of the community. It enables villages, cities, states, as well as individuals and corporations to *go ahead* immediately with public works and improvements *as if* the actual gold dollars were tied up *idle* in the treasury, because everybody knows that from time to time as the money is needed it will be forthcoming, and until it is needed it will remain productively employed in other ways.

The day laborer who has a hundred dollars in a bank is an essential factor in this mighty credit machinery.

He, too, participates in syndicates. He does not sign the agreement himself, but it is his deposit together with others that enables the bank to agree to take bonds.

A bank and a rich man perform very much the same economic functions. Both are *rich,* both have *credit*.

The rich man accumulates his wealth by individual savings and investments.

The resources of the bank are made up principally of deposits, secondly of profits.

Through the operation of the bank wherein he has his small deposit the poor man is a capitalist, a bondholder, a syndicate member, and so on. He is doing his share toward the development of the country, he is keeping his surplus earnings productively employed.

❖ ❖ ❖

The law governing postal savings — deposits in post offices — wisely provides that the post offices shall deposit the money in banks. Why? Because while it is easy enough for postmasters to *receive* money it is *not practicable* for them to *loan* and *invest* it.

The *wise* loaning and *investment* of money requires expert knowledge and judgment of the highest character, therefore the government *receives* the money of the people but *immediately deposits* it in banks so that it may be loaned, invested, and kept productively employed.

On first impression it may not be entirely clear to the casual reader that when a man or a bank *buys* stocks, bonds, notes, mortgages, that have been first purchased by others the money is *invested productively.*

True the farmer who gave the note or the company that issued the bonds gets no more money as note and bonds are resold and change ownership from time to time; the economic effect of the change is that one owner of the securities takes the place of another owner, and the money the seller had invested is *released* for other purposes; he may invest it productively or waste it, that is a *new* transaction, the investment in the old remains the same, it is represented by the note or bond, or share of stock and whoever owns that is the *actual* investor in that particular enterprise.

❖ ❖ ❖

All his life Marshall Field did three things:

He worked very hard.

He spent very little on himself.

He invested his savings and income as rapidly as possible.

He was a very efficient *human machine* for the production of wealth. As such he was an exceedingly valuable member of society, so valuable that any socialistic community could afford to pay him for his services a salary much larger than the amount he annually spent on himself.

But it will be urged that, conceding his genius as a merchant and his value to society as an organizer, the fortune he made was out of all proportion to his worth, that a fortune of one hundred and fifty millions is so grossly excessive as to demonstrate on its face that something is wrong with the machinery of *distribution*.

All of which brings us back to where we started, namely an analysis of this fortune to ascertain just how much of it was *really his* when he died, for it must not be overlooked that when we speak of the death of a rich man we always say, " He *left* so many millions."

" Left " them where ?   At the edge of the grave ?   In his pocket-book ?

Why, no.

He left his millions exactly where they had been for months or years, *in the hands of others* who are using them *productively*.

His *ownership* was the *legal right* to draw from his business and investments (a) each year his entire income and at any time, (b) the entire principal, and (theoretically) do with both income and principal as he pleased.

When he died he left ten millions to the Field Museum in Chicago and a few other comparatively small bequests. Almost his entire fortune he tied up in trust for many years for his grandsons. In short he did all he could legally to *continue* his fortune in the same productive enterprises. He did not propose to permit his descendants, relatives, or anyone else to *with-*

draw his fortune; he did not want them to be in a position where they could exercise any actual *ownership,* only legal rights over his investments.

The trust he created by will prevents his grandsons from inheriting the property and exercising any real control over the business of Marshall Field & Co. until they are fifty years of age. This successful attempt to " tie up " property so shocked the legislature of the state of Illinois, it immediately passed a law limiting the power of an individual to create by deed or will a trust for longer than the limited period named in the statute. Such a law may be sound, *but not* for the reasons commonly urged in support of it. A very good argument could be made in favor of *encouraging* the individual to " tie up " his fortune in the productive industries in which it is employed, and curtail the power of his heirs to withdraw it and spend it.

Press and public thoughtlessly applauded the disposition of the Sage fortune — its withdrawal from productive uses and devotion to philanthropic; they equally thoughtlessly condemned the Field will which kept the Field fortune productively employed.

As said in passing the creation of long-time trusts is open to objections from an entirely different angle, but that is a discussion outside the scope of this book.

Socialists and communists take the legal proposition that a man may do as he pleases with his own — which proposition as a matter of fact and law has its limitations — and they base their objections to private ownership of capital upon the assumption that men habitually exercise that supposed right and actually withdraw and consume what the law says belongs to them.

If this were true the world would not be where it is, but somewhere back in the Bronze or Stone Age. If men from the very beginning had not been in the habit of leaving most of what they produce in their industries little progress would have been made in wealth or civilization, and the more a man produces, the greater his genius for organization and production, the more he invests and reinvests his earnings—the smaller and smaller the percentage he spends on himself.

❖   ❖   ❖

It will be urged that, assuming most men do leave their earnings in their business, and let their wealth accumulate for the most part on paper, drawing out and using very little, the time will come when some son, or relative, will see fit to exercise his *legal rights* and spend his income, possibly his principal, so that after all he proves to be the real owner, not the public.

No—the conclusion does not follow.

If a man arbitrarily shuts down and wipes out of existence the business he owns, destroying everything of value connected with it, he would thereby demonstrate his real ownership, but in so demonstrating his legal right to do as he pleased with his own, it is obvious, he would *ipso facto* destroy the *right itself,* since the legal right has no existence theoretically or actually save in connection with the property being destroyed, as that disappears the right disappears.

Furthermore, long before he would succeed

in fully demonstrating his absolute ownership the public would intervene either on its own motion or at the request of relatives and appoint guardians or conservators to preserve the property.

Only an insane man would set out to demonstrate his absolute ownership of property by destroying it.

❖ ❖ ❖

Ordinarily the demonstration takes one of two forms — sometimes both:

1. The improvident son or relative begins to withdraw the income and principal and use it in luxurious living, spending recklessly and extravagantly for his own enjoyment. The industry of business may be cramped, even crippled as capital is withdrawn, it may even fail, but ordinarily it passes into the hands of others and continues.

This form of assertion of private ownership is the most obnoxious; it is, as already noted, the form that does so much to bring private property into disrepute; it furnishes the socialist and the communist with striking illustrations for arguments that are fundamentally unsound. And it is this form of assertion of private ownership that will be curbed some day without disturbing rights that are incentives to productive effort and beneficial to the community.

2. For the most part private ownership of capital is asserted by withdrawing income and principal from one enterprise and investing in another. For instance instead of leaving all its earnings in the dry-goods business, Mr. Field would take a large share of his income from that source and invest it in other enterprises; if he bought railroad stocks or bonds it meant that his money was used to develop facilities for transportation, etc.

But suppose there comes a time when some-one of less sagacity withdraws income and principal from productive enterprises and invests in unproductive — the community is a loser.

"The community would not have done that if it had been *really* the owner," someone urges.

Possibly — yet the community is not a loser

in the sense it is when the money is wasted in
riotous living. An entire fortune may be lost
in unproductive enterprises, in sinking oil wells
that never flow, in opening mines that contain
no gold, in starting factories that do not pay;
the individual may transfer his hundred millions to others in these different ways, and the
community may be the loser to the extent that
labor and capital are consumed in ways that
yield no return; but it may be a gainer to the
extent the vast expenditure teaches certain les-
sons, demonstrates the uselessness of doing
certain things in certain places or in certain
ways. It goes without saying that every progressive community—whether socialistic or
individualistic—must spend vast sums in experiments that prove unproductive, in developing inventions and ideas that turn out worthless, in searching for iron, oil, coal, in places
where there is none; in starting factories in
localities where they will not succeed. Not to
do all these things would imply the prescience
of the Almighty.

As it is, this work is largely done by men
whose incomes are so large they are willing to

take chances. The socialistic community would have to make the same experiments, take at least some of the same chances, or stand still. The individual is a much better and more reckless gambler with Fortune than any socialistic community would be, hence the unparalleled exploitation of the earth, and production of wealth, under private ownership.

The fortune a man accumulates by leaving all his earnings in enterprises that are highly productive, may be dissipated in a generation by attempts — and wise attempts at that — to open up new oil fields, new enterprises, that in the end prove unproductive.

It is not infrequently the case that these new investments prove unproductive only long enough to bankrupt the man who starts them, but after his millions are all in and lost to him, the enterprises in the hands of others and with additional capital prove highly productive. Many a railroad in this country has lost every dollar its first stockholders put in, to make, after foreclosure and reorganization, fortunes for its second lot of owners.

The wealth of the United States is estimated at one hundred and thirty billions of dollars, most of which is " private property."

The annual increase is over two billions — $2,000,000,000. That is our net annual income — the sum total of the net incomes of all individuals.

That is the amount the nation is laying up annually after all waste, all foolish and reckless consumption of wealth is taken care of. It is derived from private enterprises — from the farms, the mines, the factories, the railroads, of the country; *nominally* it is nearly all *privately* owned, in reality it is as much engaged in the service of the community as if the legal title were in the community, and the service is far more efficient, far more progressive, far more venturesome — because the incentive to individual initiative and effort is greater — than if all capital were actually controlled by public employees.

In 1910 there were 216,262 manufacturing establishments turning out over fourteen billions of dollars worth of products.

These establishments are privately owned,

and theoretically the owners have the *legal* right to shut down every one and stop in a day the production of the fourteen billions of goods, but *they never have done that and never will;* they never have exercised and never will exercise their legal right; if they attempted to the community would instantly intervene and deny the right, just as it now intervenes in coal strikes and denies the right of coal companies to do as they please, just as *in the near future the community will intervene in every threatened strike and deny the right of both employers and employees to do as they please.*

❖   ❖   ❖

There are over six millions of farms in the United States with a value — land and buildings — of over thirty-five billions of dollars.

All this is nominally owned by individuals, and *legally* each man is commonly supposed to have the right to destroy his buildings and let his farm go to waste, but that is an idle assertion of a " right " that does not exist except in the imagination. It is a " right " to juggle with in socialistic and communistic denunciation, but it is a "thing of straw" easily battered to chaff.

One generation of farmers succeeds another, and each works, not to spend on itself, but to accumulate for the succeeding.

Here and there a farmer, like a manufacturer, or a merchant, may assert his private ownership, his "right to do as he pleases with his own," and spend recklessly until penniless, but these exceptions are so rare they are conspicuous and attract attention out of all proportion to their numbers.

The overwhelming majority of farmers, like men in all other walks of life, *work for the future,* work for the generations to come, work, in short, for the community far more untiringly and unselfishly than they would if all their lands and buildings were owned by the community and they were simply so many employees.

VII

THE CARNEGIE FORTUNE

When Andrew Carnegie sold the interests he controlled in the Carnegie Company to the U. S. Steel Corporation he received $303,000,-000 in bonds.

Assuming the bonds were issued, as usual, in amounts of $1,000, he received three hundred and three thousand *pieces of paper*.

What actually happened at *the moment of transfer* was that Mr. Carnegie *retired* from active interest in the steel business and others took his place — let us say he then and there *died* to the steel business — that was all.

Not a dollar of actual wealth was disturbed. Not a pound of metal was affected.

Whether his successors have operated the business as well and as productively as he did is a practical but entirely different question.

We are here interested in the effect of the sale upon the *distribution of wealth*.

Obviously the printing of the bonds *created no new tangible wealth*. The *actual* wealth of the Carnegie Company, its mines, its furnaces, its mills, etc., were not affected by the bond issue.

But, *not long after* the transaction things began to happen that did and do affect the community.

❖   ❖   ❖

During his long connection with the Carnegie Company, Mr. Carnegie devoted practically all his *time* and all his *earnings* and *profits* to developing the industry.   He was literally a slave to the business.

So long as his profits and earnings were *reinvested* in the industry, the *cost* to the community of his exceptional services and abilities was simply the comparatively small amount he spent each year upon himself and family.

To be sure his *fortune* was increasing rapidly; that is the *value* of his *stock* in the *company* — represented by certificates, pieces of paper — was increasing, but *so long* as his fortune remained invested in the business and *so long* as he drew out only a small amount for living expenses he was *rich* only in the sense that he had the *legal right* to take his interest

— i. e., a certain amount of actual wealth — out of the industry and do with it as he pleased.[1]

If, instead of selling out, Mr. Carnegie had retired in favor of a son, leaving his interest in the business, and the son had gone on devoting all his energies to the industry, the net result to the country would be first the services of the father, then the services of the son, all at the *cost* of what both drew out to spend on themselves.

And this might go on from generation to generation *until* the family decided to *withdraw* its investment, whereupon both the *industry* and the *community* would be *very materially* affected.

❖ ❖ ❖

One reason why so many English firms and companies operate at a low cost and are on such sound footing, is because the families who

---

[1] This " as he pleased " is always with certain limitations. As already noted the community at the request of relatives, friends, or even on its own initiative is quick to interfere if a man shows a disposition recklessly to squander his fortune. The interference is always on the ground that the man is not competent to manage " his own " affairs — a very distinct assertion of the superior right of the community.

" own " them *work for them* generation after generation, drawing out only sufficient for what an American would consider very meager living expenses.

These families say they " own " the industries. In reality the industries own them.

I have in mind one of the large establishments in England that has been in one family many generations. The present generation lives more simply and feels poorer than the last because they pour more and more of their profits into extensions and improvements and draw out less and less. In short the nation is paying this family less and less to manage this one large enterprise.

Comparatively few American industries pass through periods so short as ten or twenty years without upheavals and disorganizations due to unexpected and arbitrary withdrawals of capital by either estates or men who " retire " and spend or invest their money elsewhere.

The interest on Mr. Carnegie's $303,000,000 at 5 per cent amounts to $15,150,000 each year.

In addition to the interest the Steel Corporation is obliged by the terms of the bonds to set aside a certain amount each year as a *sinking fund* with which to pay the principal of the bonds at maturity.

The *total charge on the industry,* therefore, is the interest plus sinking fund which must be paid out of earnings on account of Mr. Carnegie's withdrawal *before* any money is devoted to extensions and improvements.[1]

From the foregoing it is clear that the immediate effect upon the industry, and there-

---

[1] Estimates of Mr. Carnegie's wealth put it at possibly $500,000,000. When he retired in 1901 he sold his securities of the Carnegie Steel Company to the United States Steel Corporation for $303,450,000 in bonds of that company. He was possessed of large interests in addition to those bonds. When he started in 1901 to endow his great benefactions he made inroads into his capital for several years in gifts to libraries, for peace propaganda, and to other philanthropic causes.

The fortune of $303,450,000 in 5 per cent bonds, if allowed to increase by the accumulation of interest and reinvestment since 1901, would amount to about a billion dollars today, but his enormous benefactions prevented this according to financial authorities; however, the ironmaster's ambition to die poor was not realized and, despite the number of his philanthropies, it was believed that his fortune was at his death as large as it ever was.— (*Newspaper report.*)

fore upon the community, when an owner retires and *withdraws* his investment for use
elsewhere is *burdensome.*

There are cases where the individual owner,
because unprogressive, on account of age, or
for other reasons becomes an actual handicap
to the business, and greater progress can be
made if he is gotten rid of even at the inconvenience of having him withdraw his investment.

While such instances are fairly common they
do not affect our argument, inasmuch as the
economic effect on the business of the withdrawal of capital is the same irrespective of
the reason for the withdrawal.

❖ ❖ ❖

Furthermore whether a man sells his interest to his partners, his associates, or to
strangers, his capital is *withdrawn* just the
same, and the immediate economic effect is the
same, though the ultimate result may be to
interest " fresh " or " young blood " — as the
phrase goes — so that the stimulus resulting
from the new energy and enthusiasm more than
offsets the temporary loss of capital, but,

again, this result due to the human equation
does not alter the economic effects of changes
in investment.

❖ ❖ ❖

When a man sells his interest in a business
he usually:

1. Invests his money in some other business
in which he takes a more or less active interest;
or

2. Invests it in securities, such as mortgages, stocks, and bonds, in order to live out of
his income and invest the surplus in more
securities.

The economic effects upon the community
of these two courses are essentially different.

In the first case it is simply a transfer of
investment from one industry or set of industries to another, together with the investor's
active efforts. The loss in the one set of industries may be balanced by the gain in the new;
the community may not suffer any loss.
Though, *as a rule,* these more or less *arbitrary,*
often *capricious changes,* are attended with
actual loss to the community because the man's
lack of knowledge of the new enterprise may

lead to foolish expenditures of both time and
money, if not actual loss.

When a man retires from active business and
devotes himself to the investment and reinvestment of his fortune and income the community
loses the man's active services in the industry
he leaves, but it *gains* the benefit of his experience and judgment in the distribution of *his
fortune,* i. e., a certain amount of community
capital — in other directions.

❖   ❖   ❖

While all men make *some* foolish investments, and all the investments of *some* men
turn out badly, *generally* speaking there is no
better known way to invest and reinvest the
capital of the community than to leave it to
the best judgment of individuals who suffer the
loss in the first instance if the investments turn
out unsound.

For instance every advanced community
finds it wise to allow bankers pretty wide discretion in the making of loans and selecting
investments, and it must not be forgotten that
in doing this bankers are simply acting as the
economic agents of the community in trans-

ferring capital — i. e., wealth — from one individual or enterprise to another for *productive
purposes.*

The law limits and supervises the discretion
of bankers to a certain extent because bankers
handle the money of depositors.

The community does not limit or supervise
to the same extent the individual's discretion
in investing "his own" money, because it is
supposed to be in an undefined sense "his
own," but in the last analysis the individual
fortune is just as much community wealth as
are the deposits in a bank, and the individual
in losing "his own" fortune loses a part of
the community fortune just the same as does
the banker when he makes a losing investment.

So that *in time* communities *may* come to
exercise some supervision over the discretion
of the individual as well as the banker.

The *disadvantage* of state supervision is, of
course, the lessening of individual initiative.

The state has little imagination.

The state bank examiner must check up loans
in a heartless manner and reject relentlessly.
While the individual usually derives his great-

est satisfaction from loans to penniless men
who "make good."

❖ ❖ ❖

Mr. Carnegie did not retire from the Carnegie Company to engage actively in some
other business.

Neither did he retire for the purpose of investing his fortune and his income *productively*.

He retired with the publicly avowed intention
of *spending his entire fortune in his lifetime*.

❖ ❖ ❖

"*The man who dies rich dies disgraced.*"
When Mr. Carnegie made public that statement
unthinking people applauded it as a great
sentiment.

In truth it is about as *senseless* and *dema-
gogic* a combination of seven words as ingenuity could devise.

❖ ❖ ❖

A man does not choose the hour of his death.

Suppose Mr. Carnegie had died suddenly
while living modestly in Pittsburgh and while
he was devoting all his energies to the development of the iron and steel industry, would he
have "died disgraced" simply because his

interest in the business was worth ten or twenty or fifty millions?

❖ ❖ ❖

Thomas Edison has amassed a fortune from his inventions and by his capacity for work. What he is "worth" he probably does not know, or care, because he is absorbed in his work and his great aim in life is to invent and devise useful products and processes.

If he should die today his estate would probably show a fortune of several millions, but would he "*die disgraced?*"

On the contrary he would die one of the most honored of men.

❖ ❖ ❖

It is characteristic of American business men to *bury* themselves in their industries and enterprises, to work day and night to build up and increase their *business — not* their fortunes.

The banker wants to make his bank the biggest in the city. The merchant wants to make his shop the biggest in town. The manufacturer wishes to surpass all rivals. They accumulate fortunes but they pour all their profits

into their business. They even curtail their
household and living expenses. Many a millionaire complains bitterly if his wife buys a
new hat. Why? Because he wants to increase
his fortune ?

Not at all, but because he hates to take
money out of his business, because all his life
he has been pouring all his earnings, from his
first wages, into his business and he has formed
the *habit* of *frugality,* of *saving* in order to
grow.

❖ ❖ ❖

Of all the rich men in the country *compar-*
atively few have sold out and retired. The
great majority are slaves to their business and
the fortunes of the great majority are engaged
productively in business.

When one dies the public, and often the
family, learn for the first time what he was
" worth."

Does a man " die disgraced " because he did
not *sell out, withdraw his fortune* from productive uses, and spend the balance of his life
in *giving it away ?*

Whether a man dies disgraced depends upon what he has done *in his lifetime,* not upon the moment of his death which ordinarily cannot be foreseen.

If a man has *accumulated* his fortune fairly and honorably, there is no disgrace in dying before he *spends it.*

❖ ❖ ❖

In fact we all know that men are most highly esteemed while they are working day and night in building up their businesses — i. e. accumulating their fortunes.

They are looked upon with disfavor when they " retire " and live lives of luxury, *spending their fortunes.*

❖ ❖ ❖

When Mr. Carnegie sold out and retired, his action affected the industry and the community in the following ways:

1. Loss of his personal service in the industry.

2. Gradual withdrawal of his fortune from the industry.

These *disadvantages* are *real*. They are
equally real in the case of every active man
who retires and devotes his time and fortune
to philanthropic or similar purposes.

On the other hand Mr. Carnegie promised
the community the following advantages as the
result of his *retirement* and *giving*:

1. The devotion of his time and ability to the
    selection of *worthy* objects for which to
    spend his fortune.

2. The systematic expenditure of his fortune
    for the objects chosen.

As regards the first promised advantage
there is obviously the important question
whether Mr. Carnegie made as sound and keen
a philanthropist as he was a steel man; in short
whether the expenditure of his fortune was as
wise and beneficial as was its investment in the
iron and steel industry.

That is *always* the big economic question
when a rich man retires from the business he
knows and embarks upon a career of spending
for purposes about which he knows little or
nothing.

As regards the second advantage he devoted a large part of his fortune in three ways; (a) the building of public libraries; (b) certain educational purposes; (c) the promotion of peace by conferences, international tribunals, etc. What he did in these directions cost him over two hundred millions of dollars.

PRINCIPAL BENEFACTIONS

Carnegie Corporation (education) .	$125,000,000
Libraries (3,000)	65,000,000
Carnegie Institute, Pittsburgh....	25,000,000
Carnegie foundation for advancement of teaching.................	15,000,000
Carnegie Research Institute, Washington	10,000,000
Carnegie peace endowment.......	10,000,000
Carnegie educational fund, Scotland	10,000,000
Carnegie hero fund.............	5,000,000
Employees' pension and relief fund	4,000,000
Carnegie Music Hall, New York...	2,000,000
Allied engineering societies.......	2,000,000

All are in a high degree worthy objects.

We say *" cost him "* two hundred millions. What we should say is, *cost the community,* for while Mr. Carnegie pays out what is legally his own, he is *actually* taking from the steel industry that much money and spending it on the projects named. It is very much as if the government levied a special tax upon the steel industry to do those things.

❖   ❖   ❖

It follows, therefore, that the rich man who is actively and honorably engaged in building up his business runs no risk of "dying disgraced" if he dies in the midst of his business activity, no matter what his fortune may prove to be.

But he does run the risk of "dying disgraced" through follies or mistakes of judgment, if he retires from active work and devotes his life to spending his fortune on himself, or in *giving it away.*

Both are *primarily selfish* objects.

Carefully analyzed Mr. Carnegie's motive in giving his fortune for public libraries was as selfish as that of the rich man who squanders his in riotous living.

It was Mr. Carnegie's *pleasure* to give in the ways he did.

It is another rich man's pleasure to spend on race horses, yachts, etc., etc.

We are not comparing the two *objects,* for

the objects of the latter are frivolous and perhaps beneath contempt while the objects of the former are beneficial and praiseworthy, but the moving spirit is fundamentally the same in both men — *personal gratification*.

Both men may have made any number of *sacrifices* in *accumulating* their fortunes; neither makes any sacrifices in spending.

Mr. Carnegie's taste ran to public works such as libraries and educational foundations.

The other man's taste runs to fast horses and yachts.

Each spends his hundred millions in the manner that gives *him* the greatest amount of *pleasure*.

❖ ❖ ❖

Mr. Rockefeller's greatest dissipation is a game of golf. He shuns publicity as much as Mr. Carnegie courted it. He, too, is giving away hundreds of millions, but as quietly as possible and in a very systematic way. That is *his* greatest *pleasure*.

❖ ❖ ❖

The public is always impressed by the millions given by these very rich men, it overlooks the much larger sum total given by millions of poorer and poor men.

Everybody gives something for some purpose.

Whether the gift is large or small it is necessarily a *diversion of wealth.*

That is the point, a *diversion of wealth.*

Whether it is the government collecting a tax, or a poor man contributing a dime to charity, *fundamentally* the economic proposition is the same, it is a diversion of wealth from where it is usefully employed to purposes that *may* or *may not* be as valuable to the community.

That is always the question, whether the objects for which the government spends the money it collects, and those for which Mr. Carnegie and others spend the money they accumulate are as *valuable to the community* as are the productive enterprises from which the money is withdrawn.

❖   ❖   ❖

That question should be asked and answered with regard to every object for which the government or the individual proposes to spend money.

If asked it would be found, first of all, that the government is the most reckless and wasteful spender of money, that it spends its money "like a drunken sailor" in ways and on objects that will not stand investigation.

Secondly it would be found that many charitable, philanthropic, and other organizations spend wastefully.

Thirdly it would be found that many individuals spend extravagantly and viciously.

But it would also be found that most individuals who give money for public or philanthropic purposes do so with greater foresight, sounder judgment, and finer imagination than any government, local or national.

Compare, for instance, the shrewd manner in which Mr. Carnegie caused to be erected library buildings all over the country, with the log-rolling methods of Congress in building post offices and other public buildings, where the *expenditure of the public money* is the prime object and the erection of a suitable building at lowest possible cost is the last thing thought of.

In the hands of the government and devoted

to the same purpose Mr. Carnegie's millions would not have accomplished half the results.

Therefore, it follows, that if the country is in need of public library buildings, the community has *saved money* — literally many millions — by having a Mr. Carnegie instead of the government distribute the money.

But the iron and steel industry pays for the libraries, *not* Mr. Carnegie.

VIII

It has been clearly shown that private property as we find it in all communities that have passed the most primitive stage of development embraces *two entirely distinct kinds of ownership.*

    1. Wealth in actual possession or enjoyment.

    2. Wealth *not* in actual possession or enjoyment.

Wealth *not* in possession is represented by pieces of paper of many and various forms, which are legal evidences of property rights. In highly organized communities, such as the leading nations of today, these legal rights are both numerous and complex. In fact the commercial and industrial development of any given nation is measured by—develops with—the variety and complexity of legal titles created and recognized.

The actual, the material wealth of a nation increases comparatively slowly, but the paper, the title wealth, may increase rapidly and in times of inflation and extraordinary expansion of credit it may increase by leaps and bounds, to decrease equally rapidly in times of deflation and panic. Against a certain industry one set of men issues a million dollars in stocks and bonds. The company is reorganized — legitimately or speculatively — and another set of men with greater vision, enthusiasm, or recklessness, issues five millions in stocks and bonds against precisely the same properties.

A farm is worth today fifty dollars an acre and outstanding in the community are, say, two pieces of paper, (a) title deed; (b) a mortgage for a thousand dollars.

Oil is found on the farm, a company is organized, and before any money to speak of is spent in drilling wells, paper is issued against the farm to the extent of hundreds of thousands in stocks and bonds. Several companies are frequently organized based on the one piece of property:

1. An owning company that takes the title deed and issues millions in stocks and bonds;

2. A leasing company that leases all or parts of the property, and on the strength of

its lease issues millions in stocks and bonds;

3. A royalty company that actually oper-
ates and pays so much per barrel to the leasing
company, and this royalty company capitalizes
its rights in millions of stocks and bonds —
and so on.

All these issues and transactions may turn
out profitably if the farm turns out to be a rich
oil field; or they may prove valueless if the
field is unproductive.

Meanwhile the farm as a farm remains as
it was before — less some actual damage in
sinking wells. The immense superstructure of
paper wealth is based on beliefs and hopes, and
made possible only in communities with highly
developed financial and commercial organizations.

Whether or not the creation of paper wealth
should be restricted is a large practical question that cannot be discussed here.

The point in our argument is that the stage
of commercial and industrial development of
every great modern nation, such as England,
or such as the United States, may be gauged
by the variety of paper wealth in use. Eng-

land's supremacy in foreign trade is largely due to the fact that she makes better and more abundant use of certain forms of international paper-credit wealth than do the people of the United States; she offers the people who deal with her easier and cheaper facilities for the paperizing of their resources than we offer.

Crudely speaking we demand more nearly the actual goods, while she accepts the various forms of paper issued against the goods.

The distinguishing characteristic of title wealth is — as we have clearly shown — that it leaves the actual possession and control in the hands of others. The legal owner may never see, nor exercise, the slightest control over the property he "owns." Those in possession, the real workers, may never see nor know the legal owner.

But aside from the pieces of paper a man may own, he may also *actually possess,* or *control to the exclusion* of others two distinct forms of wealth:

1. *LAND*

2. *LUXURIES*

A man's *real* wealth is measured by the

things — food, clothing, houses, land, etc. — that he *controls for himself to the exclusion of others.*

The *only inequalities* in the distribution of wealth that are of any *irritating* significance are those of *enjoyment to the exclusion of others.*

That idea must be clearly comprehended.

If a multi-millionaire like Russell Sage lives as simply as a workingman, obviously he is *not* a millionaire in the sense of a man like William Waldorf Astor who buys estates in England and spends enough money socially and politically to get himself created a peer.

Aesthetically and socially Astor may be a useful factor, but economically Sage was incomparably more valuable.

❖ ❖ ❖

In *land* and *luxuries* there is a large control to the exclusion of the masses, and it is this exclusion that furnishes the *real* basis for whatever discontent there is over the distribution of wealth.

The *nominal* basis is the *statistical* — that is the enormous disparity there *seems* to be between the man who has only his wages or his salary and the man who has a million or a billion, but the man who has a good salary may spend more on himself than the man who has a million in stocks and bonds.

❖ ❖ ❖

We will proceed now to the consideration of the two forms of wealth that men commonly do control to the exclusion of others, and try to see to what extent this control should be limited.

This theoretically true proposition will clear the way:

If all control of wealth to the exclusion of others were abolished so that all individuals were on a footing of substantial equality as regards food, clothing, houses, surroundings, advantages, pleasures, etc., no one would have the slightest concern regarding the accumulation and distribution of paper titles. A man might have a million or a billion in stocks and bonds, but so far as any material or other advantage to him or his children over the rest of the community is concerned, he would have none.

The trouble starts when a man begins to turn his paper wealth into forms of property and pleasures that others cannot have or enjoy — *concrete inequalities* begin to appear.

IX

Private property in land is an incentive and, like private property in moveables, its *only justification* is that it is an incentive to production and progress.

In so far as it ceases to be an incentive to precisely that extent does it cease to be justifiable.

The average man—in fact nearly every writer on the subject—is quick to admit a man's "right" to the fruits of his labor, to what he grows, gathers, or makes with his own hands, while many men and many writers deny a man's "right" to the exclusive possession of the soil or other natural advantages. They may admit its expediency usually under the excuse of social conditions more or less imperfect, but they deny the "right."

❖ ❖ ❖

So far as either abstract or concrete "right" is concerned, there is no distinction between the right to own and hold land and the right to own and hold what one grows on the land,

174

or makes from natural products and materials.

In both classes of property the " right " is neither more nor less than social convention guarded by law on the theory that such rights best promote social welfare.

The " rights " are not precisely the same. Society in its laws and customs recognizes and establishes many distinctions between *personal* property rights and *real* property rights. Generally speaking the latter are more restricted —less absolute, so to speak. The two classes of rights are so distinct the law student is obliged to take two courses of study, one devoted to *realty,* the other to *personalty,* and even then he will know little or nothing regarding the law of timber, mineral oil, and water power rights — all important variations of land ownership.

❖ ❖ ❖

Land rights are personal-property rights in another important feature.

They are evidenced by *paper titles*.

One man may occupy and work a piece of land that is " owned " by another. The so-called " owner " simply holds the paper title.

The " absentee " landlord who is so bitterly denounced in many quarters, is the " absentee " stockholder in another guise — or rather the same man holding differently printed pieces of paper.

❖ ❖ ❖

Once get and keep clearly in mind that *all* property rights are recognized and established simply as *incentives,* simply and solely on the theory that they best promote individual and social welfare, our attitude toward them changes immediately, and we are in a position to discuss each right, not as a burning outrage against mankind, but *on its merits as an expedient* that may be modified or abandoned at will, and that is certain to undergo modifications in time.

Looking at the broad subject of private property in land and natural resources in a dispassionate manner, it does differ in certain important characteristics from private property in moveables.

❖ ❖ ❖

It is possible under existing laws and conditions for any individual to " own " and hold to the *exclusion of others,* land to the value of many millions.

An individual may own and hold without working thousands and thousands of acres of farming, timber, coal, oil, and mineral lands.

A man may be an actual millionaire in land, but land is the only form of wealth that may be held to the *exclusion of others* without *deterioration* in value.[1]

Without any effort on his part a man may become a millionaire by the mere increase in value — the unearned increment — of vacant city property, or of farming land, or of timber, coal, oil, and mineral properties.

❖ ❖ ❖

In so far as private property in land is an

---

[1] A man might hoard many thousands in gold, or even in coal or wheat, to the exclusion of others, letting the gold lie idle and the wheat and coal perish, but this course would be so unusual, his family or the state would interfere on the ground he was not sane. Furthermore if any number of rich men did such things laws would be speedily passed to prevent the withdrawing of actual wealth from productive uses, and hoarding it; in other words the millionaire is permitted the satisfaction of *thinking* himself rich *so long* as he does not attempt to withdraw his wealth from where it is productively employed by others. He can accumulate his pieces of paper undisturbed so long as others — and through them the community — have the real use and enjoyment of his wealth.

incentive to greater *productive effort* it is a benefit, but when it fails to act as such incentive it should be limited accordingly.

It is *significant* how often and at how many different angles we come against property in land as the one *stubborn proposition* in every attempt to work out a solution of the problem of the just distribution of wealth.

It is the *most stubborn* factor in social economy, and until it is *understood* and *rightly dealt* with, it will block every effort toward reform of economic conditions.

❖ ❖ ❖

The proposition that, aside from land-owners, there are few *actual* millionaires, may seem startling, but it is *true*.

However widely this little book may be read, not a reader will be able to name a man — aside from land-owners — who has at any given moment the *actual* and *exclusive* possession of a million dollars of wealth.

If you name a man who " owns " an immense factory, the factory is in the actual possession and control of his employees, *they* are operating it primarily for their own benefit, second-

arily for his, in reality for the community. If
he dies suddenly the factory goes on the same.
If the government should buy or confiscate it,
work would go right on. If he sells, the employee may not know it for weeks or months.

❖ ❖ ❖

If you point to a rich man's home, it is true
it may have cost a million dollars, but in just
what *sense* is it *his?*

The labor of the community built and fur-
nished it, just as it built the public library in
the next block.

Assume for the sake of the argument the
two buildings in outward appearance are exact
duplicates and equally ornamental to the street,
then so far as improvement of the street is
concerned one is as valuable to the community
as the other.

True the library is incomparably the more
useful, but the millionaire does not live *alone,*
nor does he exclude the public entirely.

His house is occupied by many servants and
employees and it is kept in condition by
plumbers, painters, decorators.

If there is a lawn it is kept in order almost

wholly for the pleasure of those who pass, just as the park across the street is kept in order to please the public.

Of the actual cost of the house itself a large percentage was spent upon the outside, upon its *appearance* to make it attractive to others.

All its costly contents, furniture, rugs, pictures, have been gathered from all over the world, not that the " owner " may enjoy them to the exclusion of others, but in order that others may see them.

In a sense the house is a small museum. It is not open to the public generally but it is open to a large number. As the " collection " of pictures, bric-a-brac, curios, etc., increases, the " owner " almost invariably seeks to have it seen and enjoyed by larger and larger numbers; he either throws his house open on certain days, thereby making it for the time being a *public museum,* or he loans and, often, finally gives his collection to a public institution.

The real incentive to build a costly home is the interest and applause of the public.

The owner may have been moved by motives

of vulgar ostentation, by the desire to " outdo " his neighbors, in short to splurge and display his wealth.

But a man cannot be *ostentatious,* cannot *splurge* without a public, any more than a theatrical manager or the governing body of a museum.

The nation *splurges* in its public buildings and makes some sad failures.

There is a strong tendency in this country to require that buildings on certain streets shall conform to certain standards of size and beauty. This is in the interest of the community. It means that the individual who builds on the street must build a fifty or a hundred-thousand dollar building, even though he himself would be content to live in a cottage.

If Fifth Avenue is lined with costly residences and business blocks it is because the standards set by the community call for large expenditures on a street so important to the life of the city.

If a man should erect a cheap garage on Fifth Avenue the entire city would resent it. Manufacturing is barred from certain blocks.

If we keep this proposition clearly in mind
— that property in all its forms is neither more
nor less than so many different kinds of *control,* encouraged, permitted, limited by the
community for *its* welfare — we have paved the
way for a dispassionate discussion of the advantages and disadvantages of any particular
form of property — such, for instance, as that
in land.

❖ ❖ ❖

Land by reason of its more permanent character and definite quantity, is sharply distinguished from all forms of property that are
created by human effort.

But *private property in land* developed like
all other rights to meet and better conditions.

Every attempt to distinguish fundamentally
between rights to land and natural resources
on the one hand and rights to personal property on the other, leads to confusion worse con-
founded since it necessarily assumes something
sacred or indisputable in the latter rights, and
this assumption obviously blocks all attempts
on the part of the community to limit those
rights.

In fact the assumption necessarily denies the slow evolution of those rights; for if they *evolved* to meet community needs, increasing in number and complexity as society advances, it is plain they may devolve to meet reverse conditions.

The literature of communism, socialism, and radical economics generally is filled with arguments to the effect that private ownership of land is in some way fundamentally distinguishable from private ownership of personal property, and is an outrage upon mankind.

Be it said to the credit of the logical communists that is not *their* contention; they denounce personal property rights as vigorously as real.

Henry George[1] lays down the following proposition:

What constitutes the rightful basis of property?

A man belongs to himself, so his labor when put in concrete form belongs to him.

For this reason, that which a man makes or produces is his own, as against all the world — to enjoy,

[1] *Progress and Poverty*, Book VII, chap. i.

or to destroy, to use, to exchange, or to give. No one else can rightfully claim it, and his exclusive right to it involves no wrong to anyone else. Thus there is to everything produced by human exertion a clear and indisputable title to exclusive possession and enjoyment, which is perfectly consistent with justice, as it descends from the original producer, *in whom it vested by natural law.*[1]

It would be difficult to embody in so few terse rhetorical lines, more false premises and false logic.

As matters of fact:

1. A man does *not* belong to himself. Biologically he belongs in part first of all to woman; secondly, to his offspring; thirdly, to his tribe or people.

A man no more belongs to himself than a woman belongs to herself, a babe to itself.

The proposition is mere sounding rhetoric, but it has worked no end of harm throughout the ages. It is at the basis of the individual's fight against restraint, against the reign of law and order that has made him what he is.

2. The fruits of a man's labor do *not* belong to him.

---

[1] Italics are the writer's.

They belong to his mate, his offspring, his tribe, without whose cooperation there would be no "fruits" or property of any kind.

3. A man's rights to the fruits of his labor are *not* vested by natural law.

As here used "natural law" is simply rhetoric. We live in the midst of natural laws, both utilizing and struggling against them, but there is no "natural law" that gives me a right to the pen I hold or the clothes I wear, the house I live in, or the land it stands on. All these rights are established by *human* laws and institutions, and each one may be modified or abolished; as a matter of fact not one remains precisely the same from generation to generation.

❖   ❖   ❖

It would be difficult to condense into the same number of words more inconsequential reasoning than the following:

The pen with which I am writing is justly mine. No other human being can rightfully lay claim to it, for in me is the title of the producers who made it. It has become mine, because transferred to me by the stationer, to whom it was transferred by the importer, who obtained the exclusive right to it by transfer from the manufacturer, in whom, by the same process of purchase, vested the rights of those who dug the material from the ground and shaped it into a pen. Thus, my exclusive right of ownership in the pen springs from the natural right of the individual to the use of his own faculties.[1]

Here is a description of a series of rights, *every one* of which is created by, and rests upon, the laws and institutions of a *highly organized* society, and not one of which is in any sense " vested " by any natural law. The price paid for the pen is distributed back along a long line of individuals from the stationer at the corner, to the miner at the mine. At perhaps every point in the line *labor* loudly complains it does not get its fair share of the return for the immediate process. Theoretically speaking, labor cannot possibly — any more than capital — get its *exactly correct* share. In what sense, then, do I " own" a pen in the production of which any man has put either more or less labor than he was paid for?

The simple fact is I have in my possession a pen — it may have been given me; I may have paid half-price at a bankrupt sale; or I may

---

[1] *Progress and Poverty*, Book VII, chap. i.

have paid an excessive price as the result of a mistake or of extortion on the part of the dealer.

The *law* recognizes and protects my possession; it creates what is called my "ownership," and it is often quick to cancel or modify that ownership to the extent of my paying over again, if it finds my title is not legal. Or it may compel me to devote a part of the value of the pen (included as it is in the sum total of my wealth) to the support of my wife and children, the laying of a walk or a pavement, etc. The community is deaf to my plea that my right to the pen and other personal property is "vested by natural law."

George goes on to say:

This right of ownership that springs from labor excludes the possibility of any other right of ownership.

The right to the produce of labor cannot be enjoyed without the right to the free use of the opportunities offered by nature, and to admit the right of property in these is to deny the right of property in the produce of labor.

Whatever may be said for the institution of private

property in land, it is therefore plain that it cannot
be defended on the score of justice.

The equal right of all men to the use of land is as
clear as their equal right to breathe the air — it is a
right proclaimed by the fact of their existence.

❖ ❖ ❖

These propositions *sound* convincing, and
unhappily they do convince and stir the dis-
contented and the superficial to the point of
revolution and rebellion against authority.

❖ ❖ ❖

If the matter were so plain as George claims,
private property in land would have ended long
ago; in fact it is difficult to see how it could
have evolved and gained so strong a foothold
the world over.

Yet here it is, one of the basic institutions of
social advancement. The logical economist
and social philosopher can reach but one conclusion, the institution must have been an
economic necessity. It may not be perfect; it
may call for material modification; but the
same may be said of all personal property
rights, for like them it is the product of
economic and social evolution.

George goes on to demonstrate by a long

revue of primitive societies[1] that land and natural resources were the property of the tribe — precisely as might be expected.

The smaller, the simpler, and cruder the social organization, the fewer the rights of all kinds, especially exclusive rights to the occupation of tracts of land, large or small. Conditions rendered such rights of little value to the individual and possibly inconvenient to the tribe. Fifty years ago in our sparsely settled western territories exclusive rights to vast grazing lands were imperfectly recognized; sheep-owners and cattle-owners would fight over them, since sheep spoil the grazing for cattle. But as the territories became more densely populated rights to the use and occupation of natural resources became more clearly defined and more complex.

George rather naively confesses the futility of his labored demonstration in these two summings up:

The general course of the development of modern civilization since the feudal period has been to the

[1] *Progress and Poverty*, Book VII, chap. **iv.**

subversion of these natural and primary ideas of collective ownership.

The reason, I take it, that with the extension of the idea of personal freedom has gone on an extension of the idea of private property in land, is that as in the progress of civilization the grosser forms of supremacy connected with land ownership were dropped, or abolished, or became less obvious, attention was diverted from the more insidious, but really more potential forms, and the land-owners were easily enabled to put property in land on the same basis as other property.

The importance of this paragraph lies in the admission of *fact* that with the development of society, private rights in land developed parallel with rights in other property.

George would have his readers believe that *personal* property rights are "vested by natural law" and are just; while *real* property rights are contrary to natural law and *unjust,* yet both have evolved along the same lines and attained substantially the same degree of complexity.

With far less heat and rhetoric Herbert Spencer[1] reached the same conclusions regard-

---

[1] *Social Statics,* chap. ix.

ing private property in land and printed them when Henry George was a young man of twenty, and thirty years before *Progress and Poverty* was published.

Spencer's reasoning is as follows:

1. Given a race of beings having like claims to pursue the objects of their desires — given a world adapted to the gratification of those desires — a world into which such beings are similarly born, and it unavoidably follows that they have equal rights to the use of this world. For if each of them "has freedom to do all that he wills provided he infringes not the equal freedom of any other,"[1] then each of them is free to use the earth for the satisfaction of his wants, provided he allows all others

---

[1] This purely theoretical proposition is at the basis of Spencer's reasoning and conclusions in *Social Statics*. It is printed in italics as his *first principle* — see chapter ix. It is the fundamental basis of *Individualism*, of a social philosophy that views society primarily and practically solely from the standpoint of the individual; it starts out with an abstract and hypothetical individual — aloof from all family, tribal, social ties — and assumes *that* individual possessed certain "natural" rights, which he relinquishes in part as he becomes a member of society. The old Rousseauan — *contrat social* — state of nature, etc., theories over again.

the same liberty. And conversely, it is manifest that no one, or part of them, may use the earth in such a way as to prevent the rest from similarly using it, since that to do this is to assume greater freedom than the rest, and consequently to break the law.

Equity, therefore, does not permit private property in land.

Briefly reviewing the argument, we see that the right of each man to the use of the earth, limited only by the like rights of his fellowmen, is immediately deducible from the law of equal freedom. We see that the maintenance of this right necessarily forbids private property in land. On examination all existing titles to such property turn out to be invalid, those founded on reclamation, inclusive. It appears that not even an equal apportionment of the earth amongst its inhabitants could generate a legitimate proprietorship. We find that if pushed to its ultimate consequences, a claim to exclusive possession of the soil involves a land-owning despotism.[1] We further find that such

---

[1] Here it is worth while to remark that it is only an abstract and *purely theoretical proposition* that can " be

a claim is constantly denied by the enactment of our Legislature.[1]   And we find lastly, that the theory of the co-heirship of all men to the soil, is consistent with the highest civilization; and that, however difficult it may be to embody that theory in fact equity sternly commands it to be done.

❖ ❖ ❖

What is the remedy Spencer proposed? Ownership by the Nation.

The change required would simply be a change of landlords.   Separate ownerships would merge into the joint-stock ownership of the public.   Instead of being in the possession of individuals, the country would be held by the great corporate body — society.

---

pushed to its ultimate consequences." As for instance, Henry George's proposition that *personal property rights are vested by natural law* can be pushed to the most extreme and absurd conclusions. The *practical* proposition that *all* property rights are in no sense abstract, but wholly the result of human and social relations, developing and changing, with changing social conditions, and at all times subject to the will of the community, cannot be pushed to extreme or absurd conclusions.

[1] Here Spencer recognizes the *practical* fact that private property in land is nowhere absolute, that the everyman's right to real estate is at all times subordinate to the will and welfare of the community. Hence the logical inference is that the community considers it to be for the best interests of all to maintain and protect precisely the rights — both real and personal — the law now recognizes.

Instead of leasing his acres from an isolated proprietor, the farmer would lease them from the nation.

Exceedingly simple in statement, but in practice!

One objection is sufficient to topple the house of illogical cards.

His conclusion and final proposition is to vest the ownership in the nation, but all his premises and reasoning require the ownership to be in mankind irrespective of tribes and nations.

The land-owners of England are deprived of their titles and required to lease from the state. How about the land-owners of Scotland and Ireland? of Denmark, Sweden, Norway, the Continent, and so on?

Their rights to enjoy the soil of England are as sacred, as "natural," as those of the people of England, and they may object to the terms dictated by the new landlord—the English government, just as Japanese and Chinese object to the exclusion and other restrictive immigration laws made by the American governments, federal and state.

When we begin to talk about the individual's

inalienable rights to access to the soil, to light, air, etc., one cannot see why those rights should either end or change at the imaginary geographical line that divides one nation from another.

Suppose each nation on the Continent takes title to all lands within its boundaries, and does with those lands as it pleases, the result would be as many different landlords as there are nations.

Theoretically just and universal distribution and enjoyment of land privileges would be as far off as ever.

George's famous single-tax plan is directly suggested in the paragraph from *Social Statics* before quoted.

❖   ❖   ❖

Happily for George his single-tax proposition does not stand or fall by his long argument against ownership of land. He says:

I do not propose either to purchase or to confiscate private property in land. The first would be unjust; the second, needless. Let the individuals who now hold it still retain, if they want to, possession of what they are pleased to call *their* land. Let them continue to call it *their* land. Let them buy and sell, and bequeath and devise it. We may safely leave them the shell, if we take the kernel. *It is not necessary to confiscate land; it is only necessary to confiscate rent.*

Nor to take rent for public uses is it necessary that the state should bother with the letting of lands, and assume the chances of favoritism, collusion, and corruption that might involve. It is not necessary that any new machinery should be created. The machinery already exists. Instead of extending it, all we have to do is to simplify and reduce it. *By leaving to land-owners a percentage of rent* which would probably be much less than the cost and loss involved in attempting to rent lands through state agency, and by making use of this existing machinery, we may without jar or shock, assert the common right to land by taking rent for public uses.[1]

Rather a lame and impotent conclusion after the eloquent demonstration of the iniquity and fundamental injustice of any private owner- ship of natural resources.

Private ownership is to continue!

Why?

Because the state could not fairly, honestly, and efficiently act as landlord!

But the state is to go in partnership with the land-owner and take all of the profits except

---

[1] *Progress and Poverty*, Book VIII, chap. ii.

just sufficient to induce the landlord to run the business — a sort of partnership that seldom means lower rents for the tenant; any more than heavy income and profit taxes mean that those who pay them will make lower prices on their goods or services.

❖ ❖ ❖

Everything that can be said in favor of a single-tax on land can be said without raising a question regarding the justice or injustice of private ownership of land. Just as the question of a tax on personal property, or a tax upon incomes does not necessarily, or even incidentally, involve any question regarding the right of a man to own property at all, or his right to earn an income.

It is, of course, possible to discuss all these questions in one volume but the attempt would not prove very helpful toward the answering of anyone.

As a revenue proposition the writer has a great deal of sympathy with the single-tax plan — almost any definite plan would be an improvement upon the hodge-podge of revenue laws, state and federal, in force in this country.

And George is right in urging a scheme of taxation on land so arranged as to discourage the holding of vacant and undeveloped properties *to the exclusion of others* to reap the unearned increment.

Not only tax laws, but inheritance laws, and laws governing conveyances can be used to discourage, even prevent altogether, the accumulation of fortunes in unoccupied land.

Property in land — i. e. individual control of land and natural resources, need not be abolished altogether. The end in view is a maximum of welfare to the community at the least cost and inconvenience.

❖ ❖ ❖

The only argument that can be logically urged in favor of broad, private, or corporate ownership — control — of land and natural resources is that *development follows more rapidly*.

Generally speaking this is true. Limit the ownership and the incentive is gone.

But it is also true that private ownership may be carried so far that the individual is encouraged to gamble on the future, to sit "tight" and wait for the community and others to make his land valuable; this sort of ownership should be restricted to the vanishing point.

Needless to say it is difficult to draw the line, and still more difficult to devise the ways and means, but the point we are endeavoring to drive home is that nothing can be done until there is a much clearer understanding of the *so-called* "rights" of the individual and the *real* rights of the community.

❖ ❖ ❖

The one great objection to abolishing private ownership and control of landed property in any or all of its forms in favor of the state, is the *poor and inefficient use* the state makes of its opportunities.

State ownership is so wasteful, so inefficient, and often so corrupt that most thinking — and instinctively many unthinking — men are opposed to it.

In short the evils of private ownership are believed to be less than those of the state. The individual may make a poor landlord, but it is notorious that the state or city makes a worse so far as getting real value out of the property for the community. The state either does nothing or is badly victimized in trying to utilize its properties.

All this may change as people think more on the subject, and there can be no change for the better until they do think more.

When they think long enough and hard enough either to abolish or greatly curtail private ownership of land, they will probably think far enough to perfect the machinery of state control.

❖ ❖ ❖

At all events the limitation of private ownership of land — especially unused land — would probably go further toward pacifying mankind and allaying discontent than any other one social or economic reform.

The *means whereby* would require a small volume; this book must be content to point out the logical *whereto* — the inevitable end.

X

Luxuries — a word in everyday use, yet exceedingly difficult to define.

What are luxuries to one age are necessaries to another; what are luxuries to one man, one people, one race, are necessaries to another.

All such statements are little more than familiar truisms. They do not help us on our way save as they demonstrate the impossibility of any hard and fast definition of the term.[1]

Every nation and every age considers everything as superfluous which they do not habitually use. Holinshed, in his chronicle, groans over the ultra-refinement of the English in his times (1577), because they were everywhere introducing chimneys, instead of allowing the smoke to escape through cracks in the roof, and were using vessels of earthenware, or even of tin, in place of the old wooden bowls and jugs. Another author of the same period, Slaney, "On Rural Expenditure," is indignant that oak should be used in building, instead of willow. "Formerly," he exclaims, "houses were of willow and men were of

---

[1] The Century dictionary quotes Cowper's lines:
First Necessity invented stools,
Convenience next suggested elbow chairs,
And Luxury th' accomplish'd *Sofa* last.

oak, now-a-days, houses are of oak and men are of willow.'' In the Middle Ages linen was so rare that princesses would make a present of a shirt to their betrothed, and it was the general custom on going to bed to take off even this first garment. It would be considered today the very extreme of misery to be reduced to dispensing with this. When flowered cottons and muslins first were introduced from India, wealthy ladies only could wear them, now, workingmen's wives despise them.[1]

As the luxuries of one generation become the comforts and necessities of the next, new luxuries are devised, and so on from generation to generation. Each feverishly seeks new things, new pleasures, new sensations, and these *new* things and pleasures are luxuries so long as they are novel and comparatively rare — that is enjoyed by the comparatively few.

This demand for the new, the novel, the rare, the unusual, is *inherent* in human nature. It is closely allied to, or springs from *curiosity*.

It is part of the primitive love of ostentation, the desire to excel others in strength, achieve-

---

[1] Emile de Laveleye, *Luxury*, pp. 5 and 6. This little book or essay, is more of a sermon than discussion.

ment, adornment. It is part of the natural desire to excel in the eyes of the opposite sex, to do things, wear things, have things that will make the opposite sex take notice and admire.

When we talk of the " love of luxury," that is only superficially correct. The true phrase would be the " love of the admiration — or envy, or notoriety — that luxuries and luxurious living arouse."

It is idle to condemn luxuries or luxurious living as such. If luxuries and luxurious living are wrong then we must seek and eradicate the *instincts* and *desires* that create luxuries.

When we seek these instincts and desires we find we are dealing with the most fundamental impulses of human nature, with the impulses that perpetuate the species and lead to all progress.

The impulse to *excel* is one of the most valuable to the race. It may appear ruthless in some of its consequences, but without it there can be no progress of any kind — spiritual or material.

The impulse to out-do, out-shine, out-talk, out-sing, out-show, out-eat, out-dress, out-

noise, out-anything, is simply the impulse to
excel in its many guises.

How tame, stagnant, and impossible the
world would be if no man had any desire to do
things or have things better than his neighbor.

❖   ❖   ❖

It will be urged that there are good ways and
bad ways of outdoing. Granted, but whether
a man outdoes, or outowns his neighbor in a
good way or a bad way the *inequality* in possession or enjoyment is there just the same;
the luxury is, so to speak, statistically the same.

So far as the term is concerned the man who
pays five thousand dollars for a fine painting,
or toward the support of a fine orchestra in-
dulges in a " luxury " as much as the man who
spends the same amount for the hideous deco-
ration of a room, or the support of a garish
and vicious burlesque show, or upon a banquet,
or dance.

In effect upon the community there is all the
difference in the world between the man who,
with sure taste, gathers about him beautiful
things, and the man who spends his money fool-

ishly and lavishly on things that are not elevat-
ing. But who is to be the judge, who is to draw
the line? More people may — usually do —
actually enjoy the poor painting, the poor
music, than the good. The poor, the cheap, the
ostentatious may actually lift the masses more
than the fine, because the appeal is more
elemental.

The big, showy, tinselly theatrical production may give real pleasure to hundreds of
thousands, where the fine fails to attract more
than a few.

It is easy enough to condemn luxuries, but it
is not so easy to designate just what luxuries
any particular people at any particular time
should dispense with.

It would be difficult to take any people in
any particular historical period and designate
those luxuries they might have dispensed with
to our benefit.

Athens and Rome — especially Rome — in-
dulged in excesses in living no man would
attempt to justify, but aside from some of the
famous excesses, stories of which have come
down to us, the life of the Romans generally

set high standards as compared with the lives and customs of peoples about them.

With all their excesses and shortcomings the modern world is better off for the human experiment of Athens, Rome, Paris, London.

❖ ❖ ❖

So much for the reason, for the justification of luxuries generally. We will now return to our line of argument, to the statement that a man may be a millionaire in luxuries, as in land.

And it is because an individual may possess and actually control to the exclusion — if he so desires — of others thousands and millions of dollars worth of rare and beautiful — also of rare and ugly, things that the masses murmur.[1]

Much of social unrest and discontent, of class envy and hatred, is due to the distribution and enjoyment of so-called luxuries — in short to what may be summed up as luxurious living.

It does not matter much to the masses who have little that a man has paper wealth to the

---

[1] We have pointed out — page 180, that men owning luxuries do not, as a matter of fact, hold them to the exclusion of others. In a profound sense a luxury ceases to be a luxury if others do not view it as such.

extent of a million or a hundred millions, providing they see him working hard and *living
simply.*

It is when he begins to realize on a part of
his paper wealth and build a costly home, buy
costly things, and indulge expensive tastes that
the multitude takes notice and murmurs, and
all the more so if his lavish expenditures take
the form of foolish or vicious extravagances.
He may be spending but a fraction of his income, leaving the balance and the entire principal in productive pursuits, yet he arouses discontent, because he accentuates the great
inequalities in the *actual enjoyment* of wealth.

It is safe to say that if every rich man, when
he came to assert his ownership of any part of
his fortune by spending it for his own gratification, spent it only on objects the public approved,
there would be very little discontent over statistical inequalities in the distribution of
wealth, however great they might be.

❖ ❖ ❖

A superficial view of the way civilized peoples
live leads irresistibly to the conclusion that in

their actual possession and enjoyment of things and services some classes and many individuals have altogether too much as compared with others whose lives, surroundings and enjoyments are exceedingly poor and mean.

This superficial impression is so strong that many earnest men and women become violent social reformers, not a few advocating a theoretically pure communism in which all would be on an equal footing as regards things consumed and enjoyed.

But may there not be serious practical difficulties in the way of attaining anything like that equality?

Is it not possible that in the utopian or communistic community the inequalities in consumption and enjoyment would still be great?

Exact equality in the distribution of comforts and luxuries is absolutely unattainable, either practically or theoretically.

Hence the differences in the distribution of comforts and luxuries between the most millennial state the mind of man can picture, and present conditions of private ownership are differences in *degree* and not in kind; the

inequalities are there, but perhaps not so accentuated — perhaps more so in some respects.

❖   ❖   ❖

Conceding at the outset that the lives of a
certain percentage of every community are
depressingly lacking in comforts, to say nothing
of luxuries, the practical question is how to provide the things and enjoyments needed and
induce those who lack them to use them.

The health officer, the expert, the social
reformer, may feel sure of the need of extensive
improvements in food, housing, modes of living, etc., but unless the class to be lifted can be
induced to help lift itself, little can be done.

It is easy to tax those who have to provide
everything necessary for those who have not —
just as easy to get the money in this way as to
take it from the common fund in a communism.
The trouble begins when the attempt is made
to arbitrarily change the habits of the mass to
be affected.

❖   ❖   ❖

The average American workingman insists
upon comforts and conveniences the European

wage-earner not only knows nothing of, but cares nothing for.

Landlords of tenement houses in this country often have no end of trouble with foreign tenants who use the bathtubs to hold coal and refuse, for any and every purpose except for bathing.

Many and costly are the disappointments of builders of model houses and tenements because those who live in them treat them as hovels. It takes generations to change the habits of peoples, to make them cleaner and more sanitary.

People indulge in luxuries before they appreciate them or know how to use them.

The average American passes through the " East Side " in New York on a hot summer day or evening and wonders how people can live so, seemingly on the streets or packed in and sweltering.

The average social reformer is for immediately uplifting the entire mass by law. The dreamy communist would remedy the situation by some more or less violent redistribution of wealth so the " East Side " would have enough to buy the things it ought to have—"ought to have" in the average American mind.

Now, it may be well within the truth to say that the "East Side" as a whole earns and makes enough money to live quite as comfortably as the average American worker—*if not better*, but the "East Side" lives as it has lived for generations in the Old Country and in this, according to its many racial and national characteristics. When it wants to live better it moves into other neighborhoods and other cities—often, however, carrying strong flavors of the "East Side" with it.

The "East Side" is perhaps the most independent and self-reliant section of New York, it is quite sufficient unto itself and when it wants more bedrooms and bathtubs it can afford them.

The same may be said of the workers in the Chicago Stock Yards district and in the great steel mills of the country. Year in and out they earn enough to live in far more comfortable rooms and houses than those we see surrounding those great industries.

Gaze from a train at the average American

farmhouse, bare of trees, shade, flowers, lawn; fences often half down, houses and out-buildings out of repair, steps rotting, porches sagging, lack of paint, care, and pride in appearance. Seldom a stone, brick, cement or board walk to roadway or barns, just paths, muddy with every rain.

The inside corresponds to the out.

There are notable and conspicuous exceptions here and there — smart, attractive houses that one would like to live in in summer and winter but they are conspicuous because they are so few.

This condition is not due to poverty but to *indifference.* Many of the conditions could be helped by just a little effort, and practically no expense, and anyway the average farmer can afford what it would cost to keep his home incomparably more attractive and livable.

The trouble is he has always lived in such houses and gives the matter little or no thought. Just as he allows expensive machines to rust in fields and barnyards.

He will buy an automobile before he will fix up his house. He can do both, and the man

who has a nice attractive home is sure to have
an automobile and keep it clean and in working order at less expense than the man who
has a neglected home.

❖ ❖ ❖

No theory of communism, no utopia has ever
been suggested that did not contemplate the
creation of practically all the luxuries now
enjoyed by mankind, but the ownership was
to be in the public.

All the illusive attractiveness, all the iri-
descent hues of the communistic dream center
about the luxuries the community will create
and maintain for the enjoyment of all.

But while the *title* to luxuries is to be in the
state rather than in the individual, individuals
— though appointed by the state — will necessarily have the care and custody, and control
of all luxuries, and they will necessarily be
housed and restricted very much as they are
now, not in privately owned buildings, but still
in buildings to which only a limited number of
the entire population can have access.[1]

---

[1] Conditions in Russia under the Bolsheviki are in point.
No end of money is spent to dazzle and amuse the masses

Suppose this country by a sudden revolution became, overnight, a pure communism and it were decreed that every private house and building containing any luxury the people should enjoy should be open to the public certain hours each day; at first the public might rush to take advantage of the new privilege,

---

in the large cities. There is a Commissariat of Education and Art, headed by Lunacharsky. An eyewitness writes of what he does in Moscow — more than the Czar, or old régime, ever did:

" In the realm of art, on the other hand, which is, or should be, far removed from the torn and troubled region of politics, Lunacharsky has initiated free entertainments, theaters, operatic performances, and cinematographs for the working classes and scholastic institutions. The theaters are thus kept thoroughly occupied. Very few new works are performed, for the members of the theatrical profession perform their duties very much like those other members of the *intelligentsia* who contribute to the maintenance of the Bolshevik régime by working in government institutions. They work automatically, by force of inertia, and because they must be engaged in some occupation to earn a living. The repertoire, both of theater and opera, consequently consists of the same old classical rut of the last fifteen or twenty years. The new new works which are produced are chiefly of a revolutionary, and consequently propagandist character, and are performed for this reason rather than for any intrinsic value of their own. Among this number are some of Lunacharsky's own plays.

" The Bolsheviki fully realize the value of the theater as an instrument of propaganda to popularize their régime. They keep the theaters open at all costs, and with this

but after a time probably few more than now would visit what had been private collections. The state would assume the care and expense of them with little compensating advantage, and in time the production of luxuries, of everything that tends to make life more beau-

---

end in view give very advantageous terms to the theatrical personnel. The latter, besides being better paid, receive larger food rations than the general population. Actors and musicians are also exempted from military service and these two factors serve to make this category of the population readily submit to the Bolsheviki régime, which thus affects them but slightly.

" The conservatoires continue to function, but the abolition of entrance examinations, all tests, the diploma, and, indeed, of any educational norm, has sadly reduced the standard of musical education in the conservatoires of Petrograd and Moscow, which were formerly of such high standing. The object of the changes is said to be to proletarianize these institutions. Education in the conservatoires and universities is now universally free, as was often the case under the old régime for indigent students. Glazunoff is still director of the Petrograd Conservatoire, but is producing no new work. Composition, except of topical revolutionary music, is at a standstill.

" The administration of all musical affairs under the Commissariat of Education and Art is in the hands of Arthur Lourier, a pianist of extreme modern tendencies who was unknown before the Bolshevik revolution. Lunacharsky has repeatedly offered this post to the popular musician and conductor, Alexander Siloti. I was unable to meet Siloti in Petrograd, but I was told he has persistently refused to accept any post under the Bolshevik régime."

tiful, would fall off; the community would become more and more dreary and monotonous.

❖ ❖ ❖

Again attention must be called to the fact that however great the efforts of the communistic state to enable all to enjoy equal advantages, in the very nature of things all could not.

If luxuries or advantages of any kind are permitted they will be more convenient for some of the people than for others.

Natural and artificial advantages will enable some to eat better, dress better, live better than others.   Unless we are to picture in our mind's eye the people of the United States — for instance — living in community buildings, *every one alike* in size, comforts, conveniences; and all eating practically similar meals; and all dressing practically alike; and all having the same luxuries such as they are; the only alternative is to picture them very much as they are now but with some of the inequalities of the present softened.

The truth is every utopian, every communistic dreamer, has in mind cities, public buildings, houses, parks, improvements, etc., etc., as they now are, only finer, but in some mysterious way *all* the people are to have equal enjoyment of and access to these advantages. That is a physical, as well as a theoretical impossibility.

❖ ❖ ❖

To return to the main line of our argument after this digression regarding luxuries generally.

The *actual* distribution of wealth is measured by *consumption*—using the word in a large sense, the sense of withdrawal of wealth for personal support and gratification.

The actual appropriation of wealth to the exclusion of others begins with (1) the *food* we eat; (2) the *clothes* we wear; (3) the *houses* we live in.

To these three prime necessities must be added (4) the *luxuries* we indulge in. Luxuries enter into each of the three first items and also constitute a class by themselves.

Only savages far down in the scale of development eat only the raw foods nature provides, or wear only such coverings as are absolutely essential to preserve life, or live in caves and woods with no attempts at adaptation for comfort or adornment for pleasure.

In fact no such primitive savages are known. The most degraded prepare their food, coverings, and shelters with the expenditure of considerable labor for physical, religious, ceremonial gratifications, and all such gratifications partake of the nature of luxuries, in precisely the sense a banquet or a cathedral is a luxury.

It is impossible to probe the term "luxury" without seeing how closely it is allied to the term "necessity." To a profoundly religious people a church or a cathedral is the most necessary thing they know, essential to their spiritual life on earth and their eternal salvation. To a profoundly ceremonial people robes of state, a crown, a throne, a palace are necessary to their national existence, they are symbols of authority, of the state itself, just as the elaborate paraphernalia of Freemasonry are essential to its activities.

As regards *food* the inequalities are not and

cannot be very great between man and man, even though one man drinks only water and another drinks the most expensive wines, one eats very plain food and another very rich.

Those inequalities in actual consumption trouble very few — except the individuals themselves who eat and drink too much.

As a matter of fact most millionaires live rather simply. Experience teaches them that they work best on simple foods and no stimulants.

However excesses in eating and drinking are fairly well distributed through all classes, from the humblest wage-earner to the capitalist. One of the greatest sinners in extravagant eating and drinking is the public itself in its public banquets and entertainments.

The point is, that whatever these excesses may be in the consumption of food they are not of revolutionary or even disquieting magnitude.

❖ ❖ ❖

As regards the second item *clothes,* inequalities in actual consumption are greater, for the simple reasons that clothes can be kept

longer than food and they lend themselves better to *display*.

Here again the greatest inequalities in
clothes and personal adornment are found in
community-owned uniforms, and robes and cos-
tumes for public and ceremonial occasions.

Individuals, especially women, may have far
more clothes than they need or can use, and
in this respect the inequalities are marked, but
still so insignificant as to occasion little discontent. The communist is against the millionaire on account of his *nominal*, his *paper*
wealth not because he has twenty suits of
clothes.

On the contrary the people, the masses, like
to see men, and more particularly women,
attractively dressed, just as they like to gaze
in shop windows and watch parades and
spectacles. There may be a good deal of envy
in the breasts of some individuals, but even that
envy has its origin in the desire to be in-
dividually as gorgeously clothed, and not at
all in a desire that the entire community dress
alike on one dead level like Quakers, nuns, and
priests. And in a sense it is this very envy

that spurs the envious person to greater efforts
so he or she may dress as finely.

❖ ❖ ❖

Much of what has been said regarding
clothes, might be repeated with equal force
regarding the third item, *homes.*

Homes are more permanent than clothes.
Being more permanent and not being limited
to the small dimensions of the human frame,
much greater opportunity is afforded for expenditure of wealth to gratify our tastes and
fancies.

More money can be spent on an estate than
on a suit of clothes, hence the obvious inequalities in homes are greater than the
inequalities in what we wear.

But again these inequalities are most conspicuous in community owned grounds and
buildings, and they would become accentuated
in a pure communism. It is a part—and a
most essential part—of the dream of the
thorough-going communist that as the individual is deprived of the opportunity to
spend for luxuries beyond the reach of all, the

state will more than supply things artistic and
beautiful, it will so far outdo the millionaire
that the masses will be dazzled by the glory.
If communism does not hold out that promise,
it holds out nothing.

No theory of social betterment contemplates
the abolition of luxurious homes and estates,
but in some way the state is to " own " and
control them. But if the state builds all
houses, all buildings, one thing is certain, the
world will lose those infinite variations in style
and structure due to individual preferences
and taste — or lack of taste.

So long as it is conceded that portions of
the wealth of the community must be withdrawn, from materially productive use and
devoted to houses, factories, hotels, office
buildings, etc., etc., may it not be better for
the community not only to permit, but encourage the individual to make the experiments?

The rich man who builds a home on Fifth
Avenue and furnishes it at the cost of a million dollars, or who develops a vast estate in
the country like a great park, at the cost of
several millions cannot take either with him

when he dies. If a Mr. Carnegie or a Mr.
Frick has simply drawn from the U. S. Steel
Corporation funds enough to do these things
— in a sense he has directed the corporation to
do it — in a still profounder sense, by reason
of his *paper* title to wealth he has compelled
the *community* to do it.

The prime object, let us assume, is selfish,
the house is built, the estate developed for *personal gratification,* and it all seems like a
luxury — one part home, nine parts luxury.

But there can be no personal gratification
without the *cooperation of the public.* There
must be a public to see, praise, and enjoy, else
the house would not have been built. Even if
the prime motive is to outdo the house next
door, the idea is to outdo it in the estimation
of the public.

Imagine how we would dress, and the places
we would live in, if we knew no living soul
would ever see us.

The broad question for the communist and
social reformer to consider dispassionately is
whether the community would in the long run
give the public as great variety and perfection

in homes, buildings, estates, as is enjoyed under so-called private ownership.

No one can answer that question definitely or authoritatively, and the debate resolves itself into a matter of personal feelings and preferences. My own conviction is that, notwithstanding all the waste undeniably incidental to the present system, it is better than community control and initiative would be. It is my conviction that community enterprise would be attended with more waste, extravagance, and failures, than individual.

The rich man fills his home with beautiful things — or things he thinks beautiful — apparently to enjoy them himself, but not so. Every rug, every piece of furniture, every picture, is bought *to be seen* by others, and this motive is often so conspicuous a man is accused of being *ostentatious*.

The net result of the building of the home is first of all the encouragement of architecture and builders; then the encouragement of decorators, craftsmen, and artists; thirdly the stimulation of guests and visitors.

The particular house may have failed in every respect save that of pleasing an owner who was without taste or discrimination; it may be an " eyesore " on the street, but it must ever be borne in mind that without these experiments public taste and appreciation would never advance. Under an absolute communism the experiments would have to be made unless the community was prepared to sink to a most deadly monotony in clothes, homes, buildings, life.

In Athens and Rome the public buildings were conspicuously successful, but so were the private buildings in a more modest way.

In other countries where despotic rulers could impose their taste on the public the temples and buildings were great monuments.

But generally speaking the *attractiveness* of a city or a country depends upon the opportunity for private initiative and originality.

The cities of the world have been built in the main by the individual, now and then, here and there, ornamented, crowned, by the expenditures of the community, or some large section of the community such as a religious body.

The cities of America are as they are, beautiful or otherwise in effect, as the result of individual initiative and effort.

Unless the people as a whole are prepared to take from individuals all control over clothing, building, furnishings, then the present system must continue.

Imagine the appearance of the streets in any town or city if the community, as a community proposition, laid out the streets and built all the buildings!

The community could not justify the elaborating of one street, or block, or tenement, as compared with others. Why should a home on Fifth Avenue be any larger or better than a home on Second?

Why should one house have any more bathrooms or conveniences than another housing the same number?

Why should brick, stone, or marble ever be used if the cheapest and average material is cement?

Why should any family be permitted a rug or a carpet unless all can have the same?

Why should any man be given a picture or

a piece of sculpture or a piano or a lot of
books unless all can have the same, or the
equivalent — and what official board could de-
termine the equivalence between a painting and
a piano?

And if in some way a city with fairly good
buildings did spring up as the capital of the
community, or about a seaport, what right
would the community have to say to the
farmer, the coal miner, and others outside the
city, they must forever remain outside and be
deprived all their lives of the pleasures, comforts, and advantages of the city?

And the instant any superior right to
pleasanter surroundings is recognized in one
man or class, that moment distinctions are created that are precisely akin to those occasioned
by the recognition of property rights.

The moment the community gives the dwel-
ler in the city a right to keep his dwelling for
a day, a year, or for lifetime — the length of
time matters not — as against all other men
either in or out of the city, at that moment a
private right is created which is, in effect, a
property right.

It is impossible to conceive a community, however utopian, that would not necessarily assert and protect the *rights* of individuals to the food they must eat, the clothes they are required to wear, and the houses they occupy even though temporarily. And all such rights would be essentially property rights.

The community might " own " every building, but when it authorizes certain individuals or families to occupy certain buildings to the exclusion of others, for the time being those individuals or families in reality *own* that building, as absolutely as under existing private ownership, and the police and tribunals of the community would take the same steps to protect the control and possession.

So that the abolition of *real* private ownership as distinguished from nominal is inconceivable in any community. And the practical questions are the extent and character of the ownership that will best promote community welfare.

❖ ❖ ❖

One man may be " rich " in luxuries, another " poor " but the distinction is less one of ownership than of actual control.

It is a matter of indifference, not wholly, but practically, to the public, whether a picture gallery is "owned" by the city or by a corporation organized to maintain the gallery (the situation in most American cities with art collections) or by an individual so long as the public has the same freedom to visit. In no case would the public have entire freedom to do as it pleased.

But it is rare the public can visit a private collection as often as it can a public, or quasi-public, hence the prejudice — such as it may be — against private ownership of luxuries.

❖ ❖ ❖

The question, however, is again one of expediency, of incentive.

Does the community, the world, gain more in the long run by not only permitting, but encouraging this "private ownership" even to the point of permitting by law the selfish exclusion of the public?

The instinct of ownership, of exclusive control is so strong that man will make great sacrifices to gather and control works and products of all kinds. Human effort in any line is powerfully stimulated by this demand from competing individuals.

The undeniable fact that unintelligent demand leads to the production of many ugly things and to useless, idle, vicious efforts, may call for close scrutiny and revision of laws which may permit too great latitude, but does not necessarily condemn the entire system of private ownership of luxuries and luxury effects.

❖　❖　❖

The late Henry C. Frick is a case in point.

He planned and built his home on Fifth Avenue to leave to the public as a museum.

Measured by the cost in dollars and cents the house and all its contents were luxuries to him while he lived and owned them.

Under his will they pass eventually to the public. Do they cease to be luxuries the instant they pass to the public?

Reduce the question to a concrete example. He paid five hundred thousand dollars for a painting by Rembrandt—a luxury by every known definition of the term.

The painting passes to the public. Does it cease to be a luxury, and if so how and why?

The time and labor devoted by Rembrandt to the painting of the picture were and ever remain a fixed quantity. Was the painting a luxury to the community Rembrandt worked in?

Every communistic, socialistic, and utopian dream tries to provide for the production of works of art as essential to the happiness and advancement of mankind, more essential in a sense than wheat or corn.

Without the development of literature, music, painting, sculpture, architecture—the adornments and graces of life, life would remain in primitive barbarism.

Hence it is conceded there are more and greater *necessities* than bare food, clothing, and shelter—those are the least of *man's* necessities.

❖ ❖ ❖

It may seem like the wildest extravagance to pay five hundred thousand dollars for a painting,[1] but so far as the world is concerned it is merely the shifting of that much wealth from one country or place to another in return for the painting.

Both Frick and Carnegie lived on Fifth Avenue. If Mr. Frick had bought the painting of Mr. Carnegie, the sum total of the wealth of the country would not have been altered one iota. The effect would have been the same as if Mr. Frick had made Mr. Carnegie a present of five hundred thousand dollars in money or in the stock or bonds of the Steel Corporation. The transfer of the painting from the Carnegie home to Mr. Frick's would have amounted to no more than the passing of a paper receipt for the money.

If the painting is bought in England the effect is materially different. Five hundred thousand dollars of American products must

[1] In the opinion of the writer it is, because it is simply the bidding of rich men for an object that cannot be duplicated, and the price has no relation to the aesthetic value of the object but it is determined wholly by the size of private fortunes at the time. As good and better pictures can be bought for a thousand dollars if buyers will seek out the living Rembrandts who are struggling as he did for recognition.

ultimately go to England in return for the painting. The sum total of the world's wealth is not increased or diminished; that could only be done if we had commercial relations with Mars and could send a half million dollars worth of products to Mars in exchange for a painting.

❖ ❖ ❖

It may be argued with a strong show of reason that for Americans — which really means America — to pay high prices in American exports to other countries for works of art in those countries, is indulging in useless extravagance, in luxuries, that cannot be justified.

Why send to England five hundred thousand bushels of American wheat to pay for a painting that is just as well off in England? Why take it from the people of England?

A reasonable distribution of the beautiful things of the world is a good thing for mankind. It is a good thing for the Western World to have examples of the art of the East, just as it is important for the Western World to know something of the literature of the East.

Hence it follows it is a good thing for every

country to exchange some of its material products for some of the art works of other countries. America can well afford to export some of its wheat, corn, iron, steel, for beautiful things produced in Europe and Asia; it is the quickest way for us to progress intellectually and aesthetically — to catch up — so to speak — with older peoples, to accomplish in a generation what would otherwise take centuries to achieve — to go on from where they left off.

❖ ❖ ❖

If it be conceded that it is a good thing for this country to export some of its material wealth for works of art, it matters little, in one sense, whether that exchange is made by individuals or by states.

The advantages on the side of the individual are his initiative and willingness to back his judgment and take risks — the personal equation. The state — like governing bodies of art museums — is a slow, conservative buyer, buying only when artists have " arrived."

The individual takes chances, supports the unknown, the radical, the struggling artist,

often when art critics and the entire academic
and official world laugh and ridicule.

The disadvantage with individual buying lies
in his reckless bidding up of prices and his in-
satiable desire to "own" for the time being
a work of art that other men of wealth and
national collections covet. Against such competition the rich individual bids a half million
or more for a painting that may have been
sold by the artist for the equivalent of twenty-
five dollars.

❖ ❖ ❖

If deemed desirable this reckless bidding for
works of art could be checked and controlled
either by direct prohibition or by prohibitive
taxes.

❖ ❖ ❖

But if all luxuries were kept down in price
to a level where they ceased to shock and amaze
as extravagances, the problem of "luxuries,"
as such, would not be solved, for nearly all
so-called luxuries are incentives.

❖ ❖ ❖

The pernicious side of extravagance is not
its cost in time, labor, money, or resources, but

its *example*. It accentuates and magnifies the gulf that divides the masses who cannot afford those things from the individual who can.

Furthermore, as our argument has demonstrated, when an individual spends ten thousand dollars on an evening's entertainment, he is nominally spending "his own money;" in reality he is taking that much from productive enterprises and spending it in a few hours on entertainment that may be worse than unproductive — vicious; or it may be so beautifully and finely done that the community may derive a pleasure and profit.

The number of wholly vicious extravagances are comparatively few — so few they are startlingly conspicuous even in our largest cities. Outside of our largest cities there is almost none.

❖　❖　❖

Let us approach Luxuries at another angle.

So far we have considered them almost entirely from the standpoint of the individual possessing or enjoying them. Let us view them from the standpoint of the community — the state, the nation, the entire civilized world, it matters not, the same considerations apply. But for the sake of clarity keep in mind some one nation — say these United States of ours.

❖ ❖ ❖

Men cannot live without

1. *Food*
2. *Clothing*
3. *Shelter*

To these three prime essentials may be added very appropriately,

4. *Amusements*

Any one of these four essentials of life may be either a *necessity* or a *luxury,* and it is obvious that the distinction does *not* lie in the thing itself.

If every member of the community has, or can have a woolen suit or a sealskin coat, then woolen suits and sealskin coats are not luxuries. But if only a few of those who want sealskin coats can have them then they are luxuries enjoyed by the few 'who have the money or power to secure them.

❖ ❖ ❖

If every member of the community who wants it can have champagne, then champagne is not a luxury. But if only a few have the means, power, or opportunity to secure it then it is a luxury.

If all members of the community have precisely equal opportunity to enjoy a particular fine musician, theater, actor, singer, then that form of amusement is not a luxury to any soul in the community; it is a pleasure equally accessible to all, no one pays or gives anything for any special privilege.

If all members of the community have equal opportunity to enjoy a particular park, museum, or public building of any kind, then such place is not a luxury, it is part of the daily life and pleasure of *all*. But if only a few can enjoy it freely and others are obliged to pay, or sacrifice time and money in travel to enjoy it, then as to them it is a luxury maintained for the benefit of the few in the vicinity.

❖ ❖ ❖

In short the definition of "luxury" turns less upon the nature of the thing itself than upon the opportunities of all to use or enjoy it.

A man or a class may be so accustomed to certain foods, clothing, shelter, amusements, that they consider them *necessary* to their existence, but to the masses who cannot afford them they are in the truest sense of the term, luxuries — luxuries to be enjoyed either rarely or never at all.

Pursuing this line of reasoning to its logical conclusion, it follows that if a community would get rid of luxuries it must direct its productive and distributive efforts in such a way that *ALL*

>Food
>Clothing
>Shelter
>Amusements

shall be *equally* accessible to *ALL*.

No individual must have any form of food, clothing, shelter, amusement, that is not *equally* available to every other individual. The nation, the state, the city must build nothing, support nothing that gives any particular locality any greater attraction or desirability over other localities. The location of the capitol, the maintenance of a university, or a trade school, the support of a museum in a particular city is a direct discrimination against other cities, a direct conferring of advantages on a selected spot, in short the giving to the people of the vicinity a very great luxury.

The extension of a railway to a particular place is a great discrimination in favor of that place. The establishing of a nation-owned industry in a particular locality is likewise a discrimination in favor of that locality. The location of a government building, a post office in a particular block in a city is a discrimination in favor of those in the immediate vicinity, and against those who have to spend time and money to use the building.

❖ ❖ ❖

To eliminate — theoretically — all luxuries, we are forced to the conclusion that a *theoretically pure* communism which demands absolute equality of enjoyment and opportunity, would be obliged to forbid the production of any kind of food, clothing, shelter, amusements, that cannot be enjoyed by *all* on a footing of equality.

If even the slightest departure from this rule is conceded luxuries appear and inequality results.

Consider for a moment what this rigid

elimination of luxuries would do in — let us say — so productive a country as ours.

It would take out of the market all those food-products the production of which is insufficient to supply the desires of all. All clothing materials, forms and styles, would be reduced to such as all could have. Forms and styles of shelter would be restricted to such as all could enjoy on conditions of absolute equality. Likewise all forms of recreation and amusements. Neither an orchestra nor a base-ball nine could be supported out of community funds because only a few would be able to enjoy either — even though the attempt were made to give any locality of any size its own orchestra and its own nine. The very attempt to segregate and support a large body of musicians and ball players would make of them a privileged class, and would arouse envy and discontent. Musicians and would-be ball players barred from the state organizations would complain bitterly.

❖ ❖ ❖

But, assuming for the moment, a productive country like the United States, manages to get its production and distribution on a *theoretically pure* communistic basis, so that no forms of food, clothing, shelter, amusements, are produced that are not equally open to all, the results would be a certain even standard of enjoyment in all four essentials. This ideal—*theoretical*—includes, possibly, white or wheat bread for all—though by no means in unlimited quantities.

Now, how about the countries of the world where white bread is a luxury?

How about Mexico, for instance, and the peoples of Central and South America?

If they are included in one theoretically pure communistic scheme of production and distribution, the standard of living in this country would be *lowered* materially. If the peoples of Japan and China are included the standard would take a drop below that of the poorest families in this country.

The glamour of the *ideal* communism disappears when the communistic distribution of goods is made to include foreign and poorer peoples. In fact on this test the communistic fabric, so fascinating when its vague and glittering fancies are confined to *us*, collapses. It cannot stand the test of thorough-going logical application; at heart it is as supremely selfish as any individualistic scheme.

❖ ❖ ❖

The net result of the foregoing is the conclusion that luxuries are inevitable in human progress. This is conceded by every utopian dreamer. In fact utopian writers and dreamers dwell almost entirely upon the *pleasures* of their utopias, upon the leisurely lives of their people, and upon the beautiful things all will enjoy. Instead of levelling palaces in some way they are to be made more numerous and more wonderful by the community itself.

But no utopian theorist or communistic writer gets down to hard facts, to details and demonstrates how all this can be done without favoring some as against others; they slur this part of their argument

❖ ❖ ❖

If luxuries are not only incidental but essential to human progress, then it is a fairly debatable question whether the present individual—

competitive one might say — scheme of production and distribution does not achieve better results than any communistic plan, and until the communistic plan gets down to detail and shows how luxuries can be produced and distributed fairly and satisfactorily by the community, the world must be content with the present *competitive* organization, *but with such modifications and improvements* as will dull the sharp corners and smooth the rough places.

A LOGICAL CONSEQUENCE

Who Pays Taxes?

Not only the average man, but speakers and writers upon taxation, assume that the burden of taxation rests on the shoulders of the man who pays the taxes.

The assumption is false and mischievous beyond calculation. It is at the basis of more radical and vicious social and economic experiments and propaganda than almost any other erroneous economic theory.

❖ ❖ ❖

Taxes are paid,

 A. By check

 B. By paper currency

 C. By coin

 D. In produce or goods — very rarely in highly civilized communities.

But while in advanced communities taxes are seldom paid directly in goods or produce, it is plain on final analysis, that *all taxes are paid in services, produce, and goods.*

The use of money, or a check, is a mere convenience — a token handed the government to
enable the government to go out and get the
services and products it needs.

❖ ❖ ❖

Whether the government issues a billion dollars in bonds (or any other form of paper
promises to pay), or a billion dollars in paper
tax receipts (still paper, but not promises to
repay) the result as regards *consumption* of
services and goods is precisely the same.

Both bonds and tax receipts are issued to
buy services and goods needed *now*.

So far as the *industrial economy* of the
country is concerned for both classes of paper
it is called upon to furnish within the fiscal
year services and products to the value of, say
one billion dollars.

❖ ❖ ❖

It is a popular notion — fallacious — that the
issuing of bonds instead of a tax levy, somehow shifts both the financial and industrial
burden to future generations.

The economic burden cannot be shifted.

If the government needs a million bushels of

wheat or a million yards of cloth the supply must be drawn from the wheat and cloth of *today;* there is no magic whereby it can be drawn from that of a year hence.

If the government needs a million men for its armies they must be drawn from the men of today, and be equipped, supported, and paid by the services and products of *today.*

During the World War the several nations issued thousands of tons of paper — paper money, paper bonds, paper promises to pay in many forms. These paper promises and receipts amounted to not simply billions, but hundreds of billions of dollars.

But did all this paper *shift* the burden of the war from the men and women of today to future generations?

Not a single penny's worth.[1]

[1] Except in so far as one country gave its bonds or other promises to pay to *another* country in return for goods. To that extent one country may receive *now* the goods it needs today in return for the paper promise to return those goods or their equivalent — twenty or thirty years hence. For the purpose of our argument international borrowing may be ignored. In immediate economic effect it simply induces the other nation — neutral or allied — to carry a share of the daily war burden, and for the time being the neutral nation is in reality an ally to the

It was the boast of our government that nearly one-third of every dollar spent on the war was raised by taxes, and only about two-thirds by *borrowing*.

That *fooled* not only the people but financiers and writers.

As a matter of fact every cent of every dollar needed came from the people *each year*.

The government required in services and goods, let us say, twenty-four billions of dollars the last year of the war.

To get the twenty-four billions it issued eight billions paper tax receipts and sixteen billions paper bonds.

In a profound sense the printing of these cleverly worded pieces of paper and giving them to the people in return for services and goods, is a mere *juggling* with *hard facts,* so that the truth may be concealed.

Every cent's worth of the twenty-four bil-

---

extent it furnishes services and goods in return for paper promises to pay — promises that may not be kept, depending upon the outcome of the war. Industrially and economically the people of the United States were the allies of the Allies from the outset of hostilities in 1914, as they would have been economic supporters of Germany if the channels of trade had been open.

lions of services (men in service and all employees), and goods, is supplied by the men,
women, and children of today, and supplied
from day to day as needed.

If a government had the *wisdom* and the
strength not a single bond or other promise to
pay need be issued to carry on any war — only
paper tax receipts.

But *financing* a war, or any other large government need, is a fine art, a species of *legerdemain,* whereby billions of *paper* values are created to be juggled with for years and perhaps
generations to come.

Psychologically this legerdemain may be
necessary. Without it the people might *realize* just where the burdens of vast expenditures
fall, and they might rebel.

The average man is quick to vote for a bond
issue when he would violently protest if it
should be proposed to increase taxes to secure
the money.

Yet in the end the money and all the cost of
borrowing must be covered by taxes.

❖ ❖ ❖

It matters not how the problem is approached the fact remains that every dollar collected by the government, whether by issuing paper tax receipts, or paper promises to repay, comes from the community in the form of services and goods.

This being so it follows that the man who (a) pays the taxes, or (b) loans the money, is only a means to an end. He does not in reality render the government either services or goods except his small share as an individual like other individuals similarly situated.

To illustrate, a doctor in practice, happens to be a " rich " man. He has a million dollars in bonds which yield him an income of thirty thousand a year. As he earns from his practice more than he spends, he invests each year his entire thirty thousand in other bonds— i. e., loans it and receives more pieces of paper.

The government in a war or other emergency sees fit to levy a tax taking *all* unearned incomes.

The doctor no longer receives his thirty thousand a year in interest coupons; or rather he cuts them from his bonds and immediately turns them over to the government; in effect the government has appropriated the interest on the bonds. If the doctor held any railroad bonds the railroad would go on paying the interest just the same but to the government instead of to the doctor; the railroad would not know the difference.

Has the government in *reality* taxed the doctor? Has it called upon him for either goods or services?

Not at all. His daily work is not affected in the slightest degree — save as discontent may affect it. His professional income remains the same.

Not until one of two things happens is he really taxed—i. e., called upon to contribute goods or services.

If the government calls upon him for (a) actual services, as it did during the war, or (b) takes from him a part of his professional earnings, as it now does under the income tax, then he is in reality contributing services and goods, and either contribution may seriously affect his productive power, in short his economic value as a productive factor in the community,

A farmer may be substituted for a doctor and the argument made still more vivid.

❖ ❖ ❖

Let us assume the government decides on a capital tax levy. To illustrate let us assume it confiscates in form of taxation all "private fortunes." Who pays the tax?

Nominally the individual who has a thousand bonds in his safety-deposit box, but as a matter of fact he has simply handed to the tax collector a thousand pieces of paper, and the government takes those pieces of paper and goes to the railroad and industrial companies that issued them and demands payment of either interest or principal.

The entire economic and industrial fabric of the community is disturbed by the shifting of paper titles, because the government is never thrifty, it always wants its money, and always spends it wastefully. Never, like the hypothetical doctor, does it carefully invest the interest and reinvest the principal.

❖ ❖ ❖

To the socialist, the communist, and to the radical agitator generally the proposition to confiscate private fortunes — private property — sounds good, and is received with applause.

Men of that class never pause to think far enough to see that the " private fortune " is largely a myth, a legal fiction, maintained not for the benefit of the individual, but as a device for the advancement of the community.

If this ingenious fiction in its many ramifications is unsound then plainly it would be better to modify or abolish it directly than to encourage it and at the same time abolish it by confiscation in whole or in part.

On the other hand if the legal fiction of "private property" is an indispensable factor in social progress then society should be exceedingly careful about attacking it indirectly by taxes which confiscate — abolish — in whole or part.

❖   ❖   ❖

In a profound sense a tax on unearned income is not a tax on the individual at all, but is rather a deprivation—a cancellation of "property rights," a modification of the theory of private property.

A tax on earned income is a tax on the individual — a real demand for a portion of his services or the products of his services.

The arguments for and against the one have no logical connection with the arguments for and against the other.